HOW TO MANAGE STRUCTURED PROGRAMMING

Edward Yourdon
YOURDON inc.

YOURDON inc.
New York, New York

Second Printing

ISBN: 0-917072-02-2

To my first, third, and fourth wives

To the President of my company

To my Sam

... all of whom would have preferred The Great American Novel, but gave me their love and their support during the production of yet another computer book.

ACKNOWLEDGEMENTS

This book represents a "brain dump" of the lectures I have given in a seminar entitled "How to Manage Structured Programming" during the past two years.

What seems perfectly lucid in one's brain does not always make sense when recorded on paper. Consequently, I owe a large debt of thanks to a number of people for helping to organize my rough draft into a presentable form.

In particular, I would like to thank Rose O'Neil and Sharon O'Donnell for typing the manuscript quickly and accurately. Wendy Eakin was responsible for copy-editing and proofreading the material; she should get the credit for putting the commas, periods, and quotation marks in the right places -- as well as a significant improvement in the overall style of writing.

And finally, special thanks to Linda Sipress for overseeing the production of the book with such efficiency: The entire production process, from rough draft to hard-cover book, took only six weeks!

TABLE OF CONTENTS

TABLE OF CONTENTS (continued)

TABLE OF CONTENTS (continued)

TABLE OF CONTENTS (continued)

HOW TO MANAGE STRUCTURED PROGRAMMING

Chapter 1 INTRODUCTION

1.1 The Structured Revolution

If you were a successful data processing manager, chances are you wouldn't be reading this book. If your customers smiled and applauded when you delivered a new system, if your programmers wrote code that worked correctly the first time, if your systems ran year after year with no bugs or failures, if your maintenance programmers complained only that their job was boring because it was so easy -- if all of these things were true, you'd probably be spending your days sipping mint juleps at your villa in the Mediterranean. Or maybe you'd be spending your time trying to determine how your computers could *really* do something effective for your users.

But here you are, reading this book. Conclusion: Your customers grumble and complain when you deliver new systems to them; your programmers spend inordinate amounts of time writing relatively small pieces of code; your systems crash, abort, and produce garbage output with disconcerting regularity; and maintenance is such a dirty word in your organization that you end up assigning the task to the trainees and the misfits.

We could go on, of course: Your programmers generally quit after a year in your organization, and they always wait until the final stages of a critical project. And the documentation that you finally forced them to write turns out to be unreadable and completely inaccurate -- so you're told by the new programmer who promptly throws the old coding and the old documentation into the wastebasket and begins anew. And on and on...

Sound familiar? It should. Indeed, it's almost universal. As a consultant and an educator, I've had the opportunity to visit literally hundreds of organizations around the world for the past ten years -- and *everyone* is having the same problems. It doesn't seem to matter very much whether you use IBM computers or Burroughs computers; it's largely irrelevant whether your programmers code in COBOL, FORTRAN, or assembly language; it doesn't matter very much whether your documentation is written in English, French, or Norwegian. No matter how you view it, things just ain't what they oughta be.

It is largely because these problems *are* so universal that there has been such interest in the "structured revolution" -- a collection of techniques that will generally double the productivity and effectiveness of a data processing department. The phrase "structured revolution" is a bit too much for some people to stomach, so we will use a more innocuous phrase: *programmer productivity techniques* (PPT). The PPT techniques include:

1. <u>Top-Down Design and Implementation</u>. The concept of designing a system by breaking it into smaller pieces, and then breaking those pieces into smaller pieces, and so on.

2. <u>Structured Design</u>. A collection of guidelines and techniques to help the designer distinguish between "good" design and "bad" design, at the module level.

3. <u>Structured Programming</u>. A theory which proposes that all program logic can be constructed from combinations of three basic forms, and that reasonable programs can be written with little or no use of the GOTO statement.

4. <u>Structure Charts</u>. A collection of techniques for documenting the overall architecture of a large program or system without showing all the detailed decisions and loops. Such documentation techniques involve drawing diagrams very much like company organization charts.

5. <u>Chief Programmer Teams</u>. The concept of building a team of EDP specialists around a "superprogrammer" who can generally code ten to twenty times faster than the average programmer.

6. <u>Program Librarians</u>. A programming "secretary" who relieves the programmer of the clerical aspects of programming, and who also controls access to source programs, listings, and other documents.

7. <u>Structured Walkthroughs</u>. The notion of "peer group reviews" in which an entire programming team "walks through" the code produced by one of its members.

There has been a great deal of discussion and controversy about each of these techniques, as we will see later in this book. Some of the PPT techniques are more controversial than others; some are more effective than others, in certain situations. Indeed, some of the techniques may not work at all in your organization.

In general, though, the new techniques *do* work -- they *do* double the productivity of the average programmer, increase the reliability of his code by an order of magnitude, and decrease the difficulty of maintenance by a factor of two to ten. We can't promise that the PPT techniques will improve your sex life or decrease the incidence of cavities among your programmers -- but what we *can* do with the techniques is pretty impressive. Chances are that if you use the techniques, you'll be sipping your mint julep in your Mediterranean villa before long. And if you don't use the techniques ... well, chances are that you'll be replaced by someone who does.

1.2 Where Has the Structured Revolution Been All These Years?

At this point, a bit of cynicism would not be unexpected. "Hrumph!!" you may well be thinking to yourself, "they said the same thing about decision tables fifteen years ago -- and who's using decision tables today? And they tried to tell me that virtual memory would be the greatest advance since the invention of peanut butter...."

Or, another common reaction: "Hrumph!! My programmers have been doing all these things for years -- I don't see what the big fuss is all about." As you can appreciate, your programmers are even more likely to point out that they've been doing all these things for the past ten years.

It's true, unfortunately, that the PPT techniques have been discussed by some -- and I must include myself among the guilty -- with a bit too much enthusiasm at times. That enthusiasm can perhaps be forgiven when one sees project after project with order-of-magnitude improvements in productivity, reliability, and maintenance. However, we do not wish to suggest that the PPT techniques are a new religion, or that they will solve all the world's ills.

And, similarly, we don't mean to suggest that the entire world has been ignorant of these techniques for the past ten years. Yes, some managers have been implementing the techniques for years in their departments; and, yes, some programmers have been writing structured code for ten years. However, *most* managers and *most* programmers have not been doing so -- even if they thought they were.

There is a much more important question that should be addressed, rather than worrying about whether or not you, as an individual manager, have been using the PPT techniques since 1965. The real question is: If the PPT techniques are so wonderful, why weren't they universally adopted years ago? Why are they just starting to be introduced now? This is a particularly relevant question, since most of the PPT techniques have been discussed in the literature and among academic EDP professionals for ten years, but have only been introduced into commercial organizations in the past two or three years.

Part of the answer is technical: Some of the PPT techniques have not been introduced because they were not technically feasible until recently. Limitations in programming languages and compiler implementations, for example, made structured programming impractical for several years. Even more important, the declining cost of computer hardware has only recently made it possible to consider the formal use of structured design, structured programming, and some of the other PPT techniques.

While these technical issues have been important, there is a much more fundamental reason for the long delay in introducing PPT techniques into most organizations: *management*. To introduce structured programming, for example, means an emphasis on nested IF statements and less emphasis on GOTO statements. Since this is probably contrary to what programmers have been doing in the past, they may well react against structured programming -- and you thus have a management problem. Similarly, the introduction of top-down implementation requires a change in the sequence in which programmers test their code (and thus a change to your standards manuals), and a change in the manner in which the system is delivered to the customer -- hence, a management problem. And the introduction of chief programmer teams implies (as we will discuss in a later chapter) that you should fire your analysts, fire your current staff of "average" programmers, and replace them all with a few carefully chosen superprogrammers to whom you pay a salary of $50,000 per year ... and I respectfully suggest that *that* will lead to a few additional management problems.

What is the point of all this? I am suggesting that (a) the PPT techniques work, with extremely impressive results, (b) the theory behind the PPT techniques has been known for a decade or more, (c) the hardware/software technology has improved to the point where the techniques are practical in most organizations, and (d) many of the problems implementing the techniques will be management problems.

Hence this book.

1.3 The Structure of This Book

The objective of this book is to make it possible for you, as a data processing manager, to implement the PPT techniques with a minimum of fuss and bother.

Our first task, in Chapter 2, will be to discuss how to *sell* the PPT techniques in your organization. Usually, there will be some resistance -- either from the management above you, the management below you, or from the programmers. The nature of this resistance is predictable, and we can suggest some techniques for dealing with it.

The following seven chapters deal with each individual PPT technique. The intent is to provide a sufficient technical overview of each technique (with references to further reading) so that you won't be bamboozled by your staff, or by your computer vendor. More important, though, we will point out a number of specific management problems that have been experienced with each technique -- and, wherever possible, specific solutions will be recommended.

The remaining five chapters discuss other practical management issues in the implementation of the PPT techniques. Chapter 10, for example, discusses the problem of deciding which PPT technique should be introduced first in your organization. Chapter 11 discusses the concept of a "pilot project" as a formal experiment in the PPT techniques. Chapter 12 discusses the problem of rewriting your programming standards in light of the new techniques. Chapter 13 discusses the impact of the PTT techniques on the classical budgeting/scheduling/control activities of project management. And, finally, Chapter 14 discusses the most practical subject of all: What will go wrong when you implement the PTT techniques?

Chapter 2 HOW TO SELL THE PPT TECHNIQUES

2.1 Introduction

It is convenient for me to assume that *you* have already been convinced of the virtues of structured programming, top-down design, and the other PPT techniques -- and that your only problem is to convince the rest of your organization that the techniques are something more than a plot by the computer vendor to sell more memory or disk packs.

This may be an unnecessarily pessimistic assumption: It may well be that both you *and* the other members of your organization have already been sold on the PPT techniques. If this is the case, I recommend that you skip the rest of this chapter and begin reading about the specific management problems associated with top-down design, in Chapter 3.

On the other hand, I may have been slightly optimistic in my assumptions: It may well be that *you* are unconvinced, and that the rest of your staff has not even heard of the PPT techniques. If so, the rest of this chapter should serve a double purpose: While giving you suggestions on how to sell the rest of your organization on the advantages of the techniques, it should be possible for *me* to sell *you*.

The remainder of this chapter is concerned with various aspects of this "selling" issue. We begin by asking whether, in fact, it is necessary to sell the PPT techniques by the art of gentle persuasion: Are there other approaches that would work as well? Assuming that friendly persuasion is the best approach, it then becomes important to ask *who*, in your organization, needs to be sold: top management, middle management, first-level project leaders, or the poor devils who actually write the programs? And finally, the selling approach itself: How do we convince someone that structured programming -- or anything that does what structured programming purports to do -- is desperately needed in today's data processing environment?

2.2 How to Introduce the PPT Techniques in Your Organization

Not too long ago, a major insurance company in New York City was given an introduction to structured programming and related techniques by its computer vendor. Assorted levels of EDP management were assembled for a one-hour long sales pitch, during which they all listened quietly and politely. At the end of the presentation -- after the vendor's representative had been thanked for his efforts and excused from the meeting -- the managers talked things over. After a lively exchange of views, one manager summed up the feelings of a majority of people in the room: "It seems to me that the problem is to find out how we can *avoid* using these new techniques. If we can manage to stall for a year or two, the PPT techniques will certainly disappear -- just like decision tables."

That's one way of dealing with the "structured revolution" -- pretending it doesn't exist. You can sympathize with the management of this organization: They were worried about the new standards manual they would have to write, the re-training that would be necessary, and all of the other organizational changes that would certainly accompany the new techniques....

While you and your organization probably won't adopt this head-in-the-sand attitude, there is some danger that you might adopt other equally extreme approaches to the introduction of the PPT techniques. Some of the more common approaches could be characterized as:

1. An edict from the boss
2. The "sheep-dip" approach
3. Sending out a scout

The first of these approaches is usually the least successful. The "edict" is often passed down from the top data processing manager (who is usually totally unfamiliar with nested IF statements in COBOL, highly cohesive modules, and the other technical issues of PPT) -- and it is frequently expressed in such hard-line terms as "Troops! Starting tomorrow morning at 9, thou shalt be structured! Thou shalt not GOTO! Thy modules shall be highly cohesive!" One such edict in a large military organization caused a great deal of scurrying around in the lower levels of the organization, for none of them had any idea what the PPT techniques were all about.

Of course, some degree of management persuasion -- perhaps in the form of an edict -- may be necessary to shake the troops out of their rut. But if the programmers' first introduction to structured programming is in the form of a dictatorial memo from a high-level manager they have never seen (and who, they suspect, has never written a line of code on anything more modern than an IBM 1401), their reaction will be predictable: resistance and subversion, in one form or another.

Then there is the manager who believes in the "enlightened" approach to PPT. This usually takes the form of mass training, or what Gerald Weinberg* likes to call the "sheep dip" approach.

---

*Weinberg is someone with whose work you should be familiar. He is best known for his *The Psychology of Computer Programming*, which laid the groundwork for the structured walkthrough concept discussed in Chapter 9.

My consulting firm frequently receives phone calls from data processing managers who say, "I'd like to put all 300 of my programmers in a class for a day, and have you teach them everything there is to know about structured programming, structured design, top-down implementation, and all of those other things. Then, as soon as they get back, we can cut all their schedules in half -- after all, they'll be twice as productive!"

We usually find that *some* progress is made by this approach ... but not much. The confusion, the chaos, the misunderstandings caused by superficial exposure to new concepts, and the unrealistic management expectations sometimes exceed the positive benefits of using the new techniques.

And then there is the approach of sending out a scout to evaluate the new techniques. Whether or not management formally recognizes this phenomenon, it occurs in almost every organization: There is usually one person (or group of people) who is the first to become aware of new hardware/software technologies. In the PPT area, the scout(s) in your organization probably began reading about structured programming in the literature in 1972 (or possibly as early as 1968); they began hearing the ideas discussed in computer conferences in 1973-74; and they probably explored the ideas thoroughly, by reading the available textbooks or attending a training course, in 1974-75. And now, in 1976 or 1977, they're trying to introduce the techniques to members of your staff who never read *any* literature, never attend *any* conferences -- in short, never get exposed to any new ideas.

The trouble is -- as is true in many other fields -- nobody wants to listen to the scout. Everyone else is too busy; as one manager put it, "We're too busy patching up the old programs to listen to any ideas about how to write the new programs." And in addition, nobody really trusts the scout -- he's brought back a few ideas in the past that *didn't* work. There may be personality problems, too: The scout may be too inarticulate or too arrogant to get his ideas across effectively.

You may argue that these examples are exaggerated and extreme, and that they wouldn't occur in *real* organizations. Equivalently, you may argue that the problems I've outlined above are the result of incompetent management, and that *you* would never make such silly mistakes. Perhaps so ... but we should remember that what begins as a good, common-sense idea in the mind of a manager sometimes gets translated into something quite ridiculous when it is communicated to the rest of the staff. The examples that I discussed earlier *did* occur, in organizations that generally went about their data processing in a levelheaded way -- but which began doing rather silly things with the PPT techniques.

I think the discussion above can be summarized as follows: First, the "brute force" approaches are rather risky. Second, there *is* a certain amount of resistance to new techniques in any

EDP organization, so it will probably be necessary to "sell" the PPT techniques to a rather dubious audience. And third, the PPT techniques will be most effective if they are introduced slowly, gently, and with a healthy dose of diplomacy.

2.3 Who Needs to Be Sold?

Before we can talk about effective methods of selling the PPT techniques, we have to identify our audience: *Whom* are we trying to convince that structured programming is the greatest invention since peanut butter? Although every organization is a little different, we can usually identify several categories of people -- each of which must be "sold" in a slightly different manner:

1. Top management
   a. Corporate management not involved in EDP
   b. Top EDP management, usually without a programming background (e.g., from accounting department, etc.)

2. Middle management
   a. Second-level managers, third-level managers, etc.
   b. First-level managers -- e.g., "team leaders"

3. Programmers
   a. The veterans -- people with several years' experience
   b. The "junior programmers" -- 1-5 years' experience
   c. Trainees -- fresh out of school
   d. Maintenance programmers

2.3.1 Selling top management

It has been my experience that top management is relatively easy to sell. Two points should be kept in mind:

1. Top EDP management often knows nothing about the technical aspects of programming and systems design -- they couldn't tell you whether or not the GOTO statement should be removed from COBOL. Consequently, they're not likely to argue with any suggestion.

2. Top EDP management is usually interested in the overall economics of data processing in their organization. If an argument can be presented in economic terms, they'll listen. If they're told that structured programming and related techniques will double the productivity of their programmers, they're sold!

However, top management in most organizations will not commit the entire data processing staff to a radical new technique without the concurrence and approval of their middle-level managers. Thus, I have often run into situations where a Vice President of Data Processing says to me, "Well, these 'structured ideas' make good sense to me, but I'll have to ask Charlie, our Manager of Systems...."

So, a much more important question is: What does middle management think of the PPT techniques? Do they have to be sold?

2.3.2 Selling middle management

Surprisingly, middle management has frequently resisted the PPT techniques. When the Vice President of Data Processing asks Charlie for his opinion of structured programming, he's likely to get any one or any combination of the following three reactions:

1. "We've been doing that for years.... Why, all of these new 'structured' techniques are really just the same as modular programming, which we've known about for ten years or more."

2. "It'll never work.... We tried these ideas a long time ago on the IBM 1401, and they didn't work then -- so they won't work now."

3. "Are you suggesting to me that I've been doing my job wrong for the past ten years? I resent that -- our current techniques work just fine...."

It's interesting that objections like these are similar to those of the programming people -- the people who actually design, code, and test programs. There's a message here: Many middle-level EDP managers rose from the ranks of programming and systems design, and thus react to new technological concepts as if they were still technicians.

This is particularly true of the "we've been doing it for years..." reaction from the middle-level manager. Indeed, maybe he and his staff *have* been using structured design, structured programming, and the related PPT techniques for the past ten years, without telling anyone -- but it's highly unlikely, from what I have seen in the average American and European data processing organization. It's possible that the manager sincerely *thinks* his staff is using structured techniques.* The organization's

---

*The Peter Principle may also be involved here. Years ago, when the manager was still programming, he may have been a *super* technician -- it's possible that he *did* use structured

standards manuals may even dictate something resembling structured programming and structured design -- but that doesn't mean anyone is actually doing it!

Let's imagine a somewhat more optimistic scenario: Once upon a time, when the manager was a technician, he designed and coded "good" programs. Now that he's a manager, he has tried to pass on all his experiences and good ideas to his staff -- a staff composed, for the most part, of intelligent programmers who are trying to do a good job. So, everyone *thinks* that they are designing good, modular programs that are easy to debug, easy to maintain, and easy to expand and modify.

Unfortunately, each programmer has a slightly different interpretation of the design/coding philosophies espoused by the manager; after all, phrases in the standards manual like "All programs should be designed in terms of functionally independent modules with a single entry and a single exit" leave a lot to the programmer's imagination. The result, in most organizations, has been a non-uniform, informal, sloppy implementation of the basic philosophies that the manager may have practiced diligently ten years earlier. And, as a result, the programs written by today's staff are *not* so easy to maintain, and *not* so easy to expand and modify.

And that brings us to the third middle-manager reaction, the one characterized by, "Whaddya mean with this 'structured' stuff? Our old way of doing things is just fine!" Indeed, this may be true in some organizations; generally, though, it would be more accurate for the manager to say that he hasn't had any obvious disasters in his department, that things are relatively stable, and, therefore, that the "old way" of doing things must be satisfactory. Later on in this chapter we'll discuss a number of statistics taken from the data processing industry as a whole that will strongly suggest that the "old way" is *not* satisfactory.

I certainly don't mean to suggest that all middle-level managers are idiots, or that they should be ignored when they react negatively to the PPT techniques. They've survived a couple of decades when the vendor's hardware was too small and too inefficient to permit many of the structured design/coding philosophies to be implemented in a practical fashion; they've survived several generations of vendor software that didn't work at all, or didn't live up to expectations. And they've survived a couple of decades when the major problem was not the complexity of the application

---

programming. But because he was such a good technician, he was promoted ... and promoted, and promoted until he reached his level of incompetence. Meanwhile, the mediocre programmers (who had already reached their level of incompetence) were left behind to design and code unstructured, unreliable, unmaintainable programs....

(most of the systems could be designed, coded, and tested by one or two programmers), but rather getting the vendor's hardware and software to work reliably.

But things are different today. Our technology is different from ten years ago, so we can afford to do things differently. The users' applications tend to be much more complex, so it's no longer sufficient to lock one brilliant programmer in a room for six months and expect him to develop a perfect system. And our problems are different than they were ten years ago: Reliability is much more important, maintenance costs are a greater consideration, hardware costs are generally lower, and programmers are more expensive.

Whether or not these comments are sufficient to convince the middle-level manager that he should abandon his current approach and begin using the PPT techniques, it should be apparent that middle management *does* have to be convinced, and that they *do* have some negative reactions.

2.3.3 Selling the programmers

Finally, there is the question of selling the programmers -- the people who actually write the programs. As we suggested at the beginning of this section, there are many different kinds of programmers: senior programmers, junior programmers, trainees, maintenance programmers, and so forth. A few brief comments are in order:

1. The senior programmers often have much the same reaction to the PPT techniques as the middle-level managers. Many of their specific objections and complaints will be discussed in later chapters; however, they seem to fall into the general categories of, "It'll never work" or "My old way of doing things is just fine" or "I've been writing structured programs for years."

2. Junior programmers tend to be less negative than the veterans. They tend not to have such strong opinions about the technical aspects of the PPT techniques; they tend to have fewer bad programming habits to break. On the other hand, the junior programmers have had *some* training and *some* experience in the "bad old ways" of programming, and conversion to the new techniques may not be altogether trivial.

3. Trainee programmers don't have to be sold. By definition, they know nothing about

programming -- and they are perfectly happy to learn good techniques *or* bad techniques. Indeed, many of the leading American, Canadian, and European universities now introduce structured programming and structured design in their first-year programming courses -- and the students have no problems at all.

4. Maintenance programmers certainly do not need to be convinced that the current method of designing and writing programs is unsatisfactory -- *they* are the ones who have to clean up and patch up the mess!

There are occasionally some rather subtle political problems that make the selling job more difficult. For example, trainee programmers can be taught how to design and code programs using all of the new PPT techniques -- but what do they do if their first "real" programming project in a "real" organization requires them to work with (or under) several senior programmers who persist in using the old "unstructured" techniques?

And what about the maintenance programmer who agrees that current programming techniques are unsatisfactory, and who would like to use as an example the program he is currently maintaining -- except that the program was designed and coded years ago by a person who is now his manager? It's sometimes rather impolitic to suggest that a system that is the full-time occupation of a whole department, a system that built the manager's career and reputation ... is a bad system. Better to keep one's mouth shut...

And then there is the maintenance programmer who agrees that classical programming techniques are terrible, and who agrees -- in principle, anyway -- that the PPT techniques would be substantially better ... but the first "structured" program that he is given turns out to be even more difficult to maintain than the old programs! We'll discuss this further in Chapter 5 when we take a look at structured programming: A program that *appears* to be structured may not actually *be* structured, and may, in fact, be worse than a "classical" program.

2.3.4 Some final comments on selling the organization

Throughout this section, I've suggested that top management may have a different reaction to the PPT techniques than middle management, and that the programmers may react differently depending on whether they are trainees or veterans.

With this in mind, I would like to make a simple suggestion: The organization should be sold on the PPT techniques *from the top down*. I've seen a number of organizations in which structured programming was introduced at the grass-roots level, only to be stymied by suspicious middle-level managers and ignored by top-level management. Management commitment is essential *before* any significant effort is made to sell the technicians themselves.

In some cases, it may not be appropriate to begin with top management -- since they will immediately turn to their middle managers for a technical opinion. Thus, the initial selling of the PPT techniques may have to begin with middle management. Those middle managers can convince top management that there are economic arguments in favor of the PPT techniques, as well as convincing the programmers that there are strong technical arguments in favor of the PPT techniques.

2.4 How to Sell the New Techniques

Having discussed other aspects of the "selling" of PPT, we are still left with one fundamental question: *How* do we convince a dubious audience (whether programmers or managers) that the PPT techniques are worth exploring?

It's been my experience that the most effective approach is a "double whammy" argument. *First*, convince your audience that the current techniques leave much to be desired. *Second*, convince your audience that the new PPT techniques are demonstrably better.

To do this properly, you need ammunition -- some statistics, some case studies, some documented evidence that the current techniques are generally bad, and that the PPT techniques are generally good. The remainder of this chapter is devoted to giving you useful statistics, beginning with some statistics on the current state of the EDP industry.

2.4.1 The average application programmer is not very productive

It is generally accepted that the average application programmer can produce ten to fifteen debugged program statements per day; for systems programs (particularly large operating systems), the number drops to as little as two or three debugged statements per day. Given the salary of today's programmers, that means that every statement in a new EDP system costs somewhere between $5 and $50.

This figure of average productivity has been known for some years, and was most recently documented in *The Mythical Man-Month*, by Fred Brooks (Addison-Wesley, 1975). What makes these figures so interesting is that they seem to be invariant over a long period of time: IBM first observed these statistics on projects in the late 1950's. They have been confirmed over and over again in major projects throughout the 1960's; and they continue to be confirmed today.

Another interesting aspect of the productivity figures is *machine-independence* and *language-independence*. That is, the available statistics strongly suggest that the average application programmer can generate ten to fifteen debugged statements regardless of whether he programs on an IBM computer, a Honeywell computer, a Burroughs computer, or any other machine. Similarly, it appears that the programmer will write approximately ten statements per day regardless of whether the programming language being used is COBOL, FORTRAN, PL/I, assembly language, or any of the other major languages.*

Recently, there has been a great deal of controversy in the area of "programmer productivity" -- particularly when it is measured in units of "debugged statements per day." Some of the commotion is made by programmers, who always remember that wonderful day last month (or last year...) when they wrote 600 lines of code. What they usually forget -- and what the figure of ten to fifteen statements per day impresses upon us -- is the tremendous amount of time spent designing the code and debugging it (and possibly even documenting it!).

Most of the controversy, though, is of a somewhat more philosophical nature. The major areas of controversy can be summarized as follows:

1. The Hawthorne Effect can become quite significant when measuring programmer productivity: If a programmer knows that he will be judged by the number of lines of code he writes, then he will automatically write more lines of code ... but they will tend to be more trivial lines of code. That which could have been programmed with a simple loop is transformed into 1,000 in-line instructions. Thus far, my experience has been that programmers do *not* react in this fashion -- for the very simple reason that they *know* that their salary will not really increase in a manner proportional to the number of lines of code they write.

---

*The significant point, of course, is that one can *accomplish* much more with ten COBOL statements than with ten assembly language statements -- so, from a different point of view, a programmer is much more productive when he programs in COBOL (or any other high-level language). The point that we are trying to make here, however, is that ten assembly language statements represent approximately the same level of intellectual complexity as ten COBOL statements.

2. There can be extreme variations in productivity -- from project to project, from programmer to programmer (as we will discuss in the next section), and from day to day. It is significant to note that most of the published statistics on productivity have been taken from relatively large projects, with several programmers; thus, the overall productivity figures represent a "smoothing" effect that might not be seen on a one-person project involving 200 lines of code.

3. Different people measure productivity differently. Does one include only the coding and "unit-test" activities, or should one also include the time spent designing, documenting, and "system-testing"? In calculating productivity for a project, does one count only the programmers -- or should one include the analysts, the managers, and the clerical staff? Thus far, I have not seen any general agreement in this area -- which means that productivity reported by company A may *appear* radically different than that reported by company B. Obviously, the most important thing that one could ask for is consistency within an organization.

We could devote the rest of this book to a discussion of the subtleties of measuring productivity, but I would prefer to leave that to others.* It should be sufficient at this point to observe that productivity -- no matter how crudely we may measure it -- is not very high. If we can show -- as we *will* show later in this chapter -- that programmer productivity can be substantially improved with the use of the "structured" techniques, then we will have made our point.

2.4.2 There is a substantial variation in programmer abilities

Things would be bad enough if *all* programmers wrote ten debugged COBOL statements every day. What disturbs us even more is that ten statements is an *average* -- and the variation between high productivity and low productivity is truly staggering.

This point was first made in a paper by Professor Harold Sackman in 1968.** Sackman reported on a study in which he found

---

*It is interesting to note that GUIDE has established a committee to look into the matter of measuring programmer productivity.

**H. Sackman, W.J. Erickson, and E.E. Grant, "Exploratory Experimental Studies Comparing Online and Offline Programming Performance," *Communications of the ACM*, January 1968, pages 3-11.

that some programmers could design, code, and test a program 25 times more quickly than others. Similarly, he found that some programmers produced code that was nearly ten times more efficient than the code produced by others -- that is, occupying ten times less memory and running ten times faster.

What made Sackman's experiment so interesting was his observation that there was no significant correlation between programming performance and years of experience -- and no correlation between programming performance and scores on programming aptitude tests.* This comes as no surprise to many programming managers, who know that a programmer with ten years of experience may have had *one* year of real experience, repeated nine times!

As with the statistics concerning programmer productivity in the preceding section, I find that there is a great deal of argument over the Sackman statistics. It may be argued, for example, that Sackman studied only a small sample of programmers (approximately a dozen people), and that one is therefore unable to draw universal conclusions about the entire programming industry. One might also argue that the programmer who takes a long time to design and code a program may require substantially less time to test it; similarly, one could expect that a programmer whose program occupies a great deal of memory would have written it in such a way as to require less CPU time (and vice versa).

All of these comments are valid ... but we are left with the strong impression that some programmers may be substantially better -- an order of magnitude better -- than their colleagues. And we are left with the impression that a high IQ and ten years of experience may not be sufficient to be a really *good* programmer.

If that is the case, what should we do? One school of thought argues that we should identify those programmers who are an order of magnitude better than their colleagues -- and then fire everyone else. In a slightly more civilized vein, the Sackman statistics provide one of the motivations for the "chief programmer team" concept that we will discuss in Chapter 7.

Another school of thought argues that we should find out what makes the good programmers so good -- and then see if we can teach that to the average programmers. Indeed, that explains much of the motivation behind structured programming and structured design: One of the things that has made some programmers so successful is their *instinctive* ability to break a large system into small independent modules, and then code those modules with well-organized

---

*Actually, this comment is true only of the *experienced* programmers. Sackman found that, for trainee programmers, there *was* a correlation between programming performance and scores on aptitude tests.

(i.e., well-structured) COBOL statements. The technologies of structured programming and structured design might be regarded as an attempt to capture, in words, what a few of these programmers have been doing by instinct for years.

In the meantime, you should recognize -- as a manager -- that you have a potential problem. If you have a staff of ten or twenty programmers, and if there is indeed an order-of-magnitude difference in their abilities, then *your* ability to schedule, manage, and budget projects is seriously impaired. This is compounded by the probability that you don't know precisely how good or bad your programmers are in the areas of designing, coding, testing, and writing efficient programs.

This last comment was not meant as an insult, but rather as a simple statement of "the way it is" in most organizations. Sackman was able to do something most programming organizations *never* do -- *he had a dozen programmers working on the same programming problem.* In the real world, Charlie works on program A, while Susy works on program B -- and since program A and program B are intrinsically different, it is very difficult to tell whether Charlie codes faster that Susy, and whether Charlie's code is more efficient than Susy's code.

Sackman's experiments thus confirm what we could only guess at before: There *are* substantial variations in programmer abilities. This should give us some motivation to try some of the new technologies that we will be discussing in subsequent chapters of the book.

2.4.3 The average programmer spends very little time programming

One of the reasons for the low productivity of programmers is that we don't give them enough of an opportunity to program. In a typical organization, a programmer spends a significant portion of his time attending meetings, filling out reports, walking downstairs to the computer room to pick up his output, walking upstairs to the keypunch room to submit some keypunching, walking across the hall to discuss some esoteric programming issue with another programmer ... and so on.

Indeed, a study published by George Weinwurm* indicated that the average programmer spends only 27% of his day doing something that could be interpreted as "programming" -- writing instructions on a coding sheet, looking at a listing, debugging, etc. The remainder of the programmer's working day is spent performing duties

---

*George Weinwurm (Ed.), *On the Management of Computer Programming*, Auerbach Publishers, 1970.

that are basically clerical in nature, or duties that have nothing at all to do with programming.

To see whether this statistic is relevant in your organization, you might spend a few hours *watching* your programmers as they carry out their normal duties. Then ask yourself: How many of their activities really require a Bachelor's Degree in Computer Science, six months of on-the-job training, and a $16,000 annual salary? How much of the programmer's activities could *really* be done by an intelligent clerk?

As you might have anticipated, Weinwurm's statistic provides some motivation for the "program librarian" concept that we will discuss in Chapter 8. At this point, it is sufficient to suggest that one reason for the troubles in your EDP department is that your programmers don't spend enough time programming.

2.4.4 Testing usually occupies 50% of a typical programming project

It is generally agreed that approximately one third of the time, energy, and money expended in a programming project goes for "design"; roughly one sixth is spent on "coding"; and the remaining half is spent trying to make the damn thing work! One of the more recent sources of this statistic is Metzger's excellent book on project management.*

Indeed, it has been known for so long that testing consumes half of a project that everyone seems to accept it as a "law of nature." That it is *not* a law of nature has become painfully apparent in some recent programming projects in which the code worked correctly virtually the first time it was run.

In other words, we spend so much time on testing primarily because the programmers make so many unnecessary mistakes. With the use of structured design, structured programming, and structured walkthroughs, it appears that we can cut the number of unnecessary bugs almost to zero. Thus, if you're spending 50% of your resources in a programming project on testing, you're probably wasting a substantial amount of money.

There's something else, too: The *way* we go about testing causes a lot of trouble. The current approach to testing in most organizations is roughly as follows. First, test all the modules in a "stand-alone" fashion; then, combine modules together into programs, and carry out "program testing"; next, combine the programs together into subsystems and carry out "subsystem testing"; finally, combine the subsystems together into a system, and carry out "system testing."

---

*Philip Metzger, *Programming Project Management*, Prentice-Hall, 1975.

Largely as a result of this approach to testing, many projects encounter the following problems:

1. There is very little tangible evidence of progress during the testing phase. It is largely during this period of time that the programmers remark that they are "98% finished," or that there is "only one more bug to find."

2. The worst bugs -- interface bugs -- are usually found at the end of the testing phase, while trivial bugs (e.g., local logic errors within a module) are found at the beginning. If they had their choice, most programmers would like to reverse the sequence -- find the "horrible" bugs first, and clean up the trivial bugs last.

3. Deadlines are often missed ... and since the classical approach to testing usually means that nothing works until it *all* works, the project often becomes politically vulnerable. When the deadline arrives, the user is usually unimpressed with 50,000 lines of code that have passed the module test phase -- but which don't do anything *as a system*.

4. The user sometimes discovers that he doesn't really like the system. We consider this to be largely the fault of the current approach to testing, since it usually means that the user doesn't see anything until he sees the entire system in operation.

We will deal with these problems in Chapter 3, when we discuss top-down implementation. At this point, it is sufficient to recognize that the current method of doing things is fraught with problems.

2.4.5 Bugs last forever in large systems

One of the most interesting statistics of recent years came from an employee of IBM, who remarked at a software engineering conference that every release of IBM's OS/360 operating system had 1,000 bugs.*

---

*See the original publication, *Software Engineering*, published by the NATO Scientific Affairs Division, Brussels 39, Belgium, 1969; or see the recent republished proceedings of that conference in *Software Engineering Concepts and Techniques*, J.M. Buxton, P. Naur, and B. Randell (Editors), Petrocelli/Charter, 1976.

Obviously, IBM is not unique in this area, nor is this a phenomenon restricted to operating systems. What we are saying, very simply, is that large programs (or systems) seem to have a number of residual bugs that will *never* be completely eliminated. Indeed, there is more and more evidence to suggest that large programs -- whether they are payroll programs, order entry programs, compilers, operating systems, or air defense systems -- behave in the manner shown in the graph below:

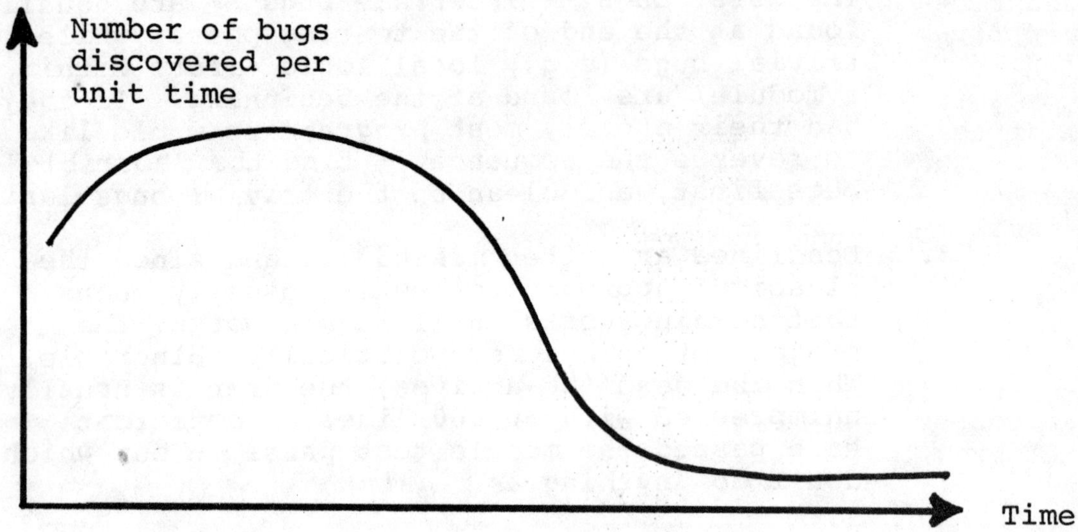

During the first few months of "production" use of a system, more and more bugs will be discovered. There are various reasons for this: The users become more and more experienced with the system, and thus "push" it harder; the volume of processing builds up, thus exposing bugs that were in the code all the time, but which did not come to light during the early "tentative" use of the system.

At some point in time, the "bug discovery" curve generally turns downward (otherwise, the system will be thrown out by the users!). Each month, the users find fewer and fewer bugs -- which the programmers fix. Sooner or later, though, the curve levels off and then remains relatively constant over a long period of time. In the case of IBM's operating system, the curve apparently levelled off at 1,000 bugs per release; for a medium-sized payroll system, we might measure this as one bug (requiring a rerun of the system) every third payroll run. However we measure it, one fact remains clear: The system will probably never be bug-free.

In fact, if we wait long enough, the curve will probably turn up again -- that is, there will gradually be *more* bugs discovered per unit time. This usually occurs with "old" systems that have been patched and modified so heavily that nobody understands them any more. In situations like this, we find that every time the programmer fixes one "old" bug, he introduces two "new" bugs into the system.

Another way of discussing this problem is to observe the *total* number of bugs that are discovered during the lifetime of a system. With current methods of developing computer programs, we can expect an average of one to five bugs per 100 statements, *after the program has been "officially" tested and put into production!* Thus, if we develop a payroll system with 10,000 COBOL statements, we should expect to find between 100 and 500 bugs *in production* during the five to eight years' expected lifetime of the system. Obviously, the majority of those bugs will be found during the first few months of production, but they will continue popping up now and then even after five years of use.

Again, all we are trying to do at this point is identify problem areas. I am suggesting, with statistics like the ones above, that the unreliability of our present systems is a problem area. Later on, we'll see what sort of improvements we can make to the reliability of our computer systems.

2.4.6 Bugs are more critical in today's computer systems

As we pointed out in the preceding section, most of our current computer systems have a substantial number of bugs -- and it should be emphasized that this phenomenon has been with us ever since the first programmer began writing programs. The problem is not that the programmers of the 1970's are more stupid or more sloppy; indeed, today's programmers are probably not any better or any worse than the programmers of twenty years ago.

If that is so, why did we wait until the 1970's to complain about the number of bugs? First, because we are now beginning to appreciate that it is very expensive to put bugs into a program and then go through a laborious process of finding them and taking them out of the program. We are beginning to realize -- one of those simple but brilliant discoveries! -- that it is cheaper to avoid putting the bugs into the program in the first place.

But there is a more serious reason for the fuss that we are making about bugs: Our customers, our companies, and our society are becoming less and less tolerant of the bugs in our programs.

Twenty years ago, a computer bug was often the source of an amusing newspaper article. One would read of billing programs which produced an invoice for $0.00 (or, even worse, *minus* $0.00) and then began sending nasty dunning letters when the customer refused to pay. True, such events were considered an irritation and a public relations problem -- but a small price to pay for the marvels of the electronic computer!

Today, though, we are faced with a somewhat different situation. Consider the consequences of a bug in a payroll system that pays 100,000 people -- in the past year, I have seen one wildcat strike triggered by a payroll system which failed to pay overtime wages properly. Or consider the consequences of a bug that shuts down a nationwide on-line order entry system, or a nationwide airline reservation system.

On a somewhat more serious level, consider the consequences of a bug in any of the computerized telephone switching systems that are beginning to be installed all over the world: A software bug can leave an entire city without telephone service until some poor programmer can figure out how to fix the bug.

Or consider the consequences of a failure in the computerized air traffic control systems that are now spreading around the world: A software bug could very easily lead to mid-air collisions, with substantial loss of life and property.

Or consider the consequences of a failure in an air defense system, or in any of the sophisticated military command-and-control systems that are under development today....

The moral is very simple and very clear: We can't afford bugs -- *any* bugs -- in many of the systems we are designing today. And, considering the rate at which we introduce bugs into our current systems, it is clear that we have a problem.

2.4.7 Programmers are not very good at fixing bugs

To further complicate matters, it turns out that programmers are not very good at fixing bugs, once their existence has been made known. A study by Barry Boehm* indicated that, at best, a programmer has approximately a 50% chance of successfully fixing a bug on his first attempt -- and that occurs if the programmer modifies five to ten lines of code in his attempt to fix the bug. If he changes *more* lines of code, his chances of success drop. If, for example, the bug requires 50 lines of code to be changed, the programmer's chances of success drop to approximately 20%.

It is interesting that if the programmer modifies *less* than five to ten lines of code in his attempt to fix the bug, his chances of success also drop -- though only slightly. Although this might seem surprising at first, it can probably be explained by human psychology: One tends to be overconfident when changing a single line of code to correct a "trivial" bug. If the bug is serious enough to require several lines of code to be changed, one tends to be more careful.

Obviously, some of the problems associated with the fixing of bugs are *human* problems: keypunching errors, coding errors,

---

*Barry Boehm, "Software and Its Impact: A Quantitative Study," *Datamation*, May 1973.

psychological errors, and so forth. However, we are beginning to recognize that many of our problems are of a different sort: We may successfully fix a bug in subroutine X, only to find later on (sometimes several *months* later) that the "fix" has introduced a new bug in subroutine Y. This phenomenon is becoming more and more troublesome, particularly on the larger systems where it is impossible for the programmer to be familiar with all of the modules in the system. It is even more impossible for him to be aware of the subtle interactions between the modules.

It is largely because of this problem that there has been so much interest in some of the techniques of structured design, which attempt to minimize the interdependencies between modules. We will discuss this at length in Chapter 4.

2.4.8 Maintenance is becoming too expensive

A survey in the October 1972 issue of *EDP Analyzer* indicated for perhaps the first time that most EDP organizations spend 50% of their budget on maintenance. Since then, my own informal surveys and occasional articles in the literature have confirmed that rule of thumb. Indeed, many large organizations spend 75% or even 80% of their data processing budget maintaining existing systems.

Nobody is suggesting that maintenance could be eliminated altogether -- but we *are* suggesting that 50% or 75% or 80% is too much to be spending on existing programs. Why? Well, consider how we are currently spending our maintenance money:

- ongoing debugging
- changes required by new hardware, new versions of vendor operating systems, new compilers, etc.
- expansions, changes, new features requested by users

As we suggested earlier, *any* money spent on ongoing debugging is too much: We should be able to write programs with virtually no bugs. Similarly, we should be able to write programs that can run virtually unchanged when the vendor upgrades his operating system or his compiler. The fact that we spend a great deal of money in these two areas suggests that we have a problem.

The last point -- changes and new features for the user -- is one that we will never be able to eliminate. However, it is generally agreed today that our computer systems are more difficult to change than they should be. A rule of thumb to follow here (but one which would probably be considered heresy by most programmers!) is: If a modification or a new system feature can be explained easily by a user, then it *should* be easy to introduce it into the computer system. If it is *not* easy, then the system was probably designed in an inadequate fashion.

2.5 Statistics Supporting the PPT Techniques

Thus far, we have understood that the current approach to programming and program design is not as successful as we would like it to be. Of course, it is only fair to offer criticism if we can suggest something better -- and this leads to the obvious question: Why should we believe that things will improve with the use of structured programming, structured design, and the other PPT techniques?

One can argue a number of points as a matter of common sense. That is, one hears the following "sales pitch" for structured programming: "Well, it makes *sense* to use structured programming for the following rational arguments ... blah, blah, blah..." Indeed, we have used such arguments already in this chapter, and we will use them again in subsequent chapters.

Unfortunately, common sense and rational arguments are not always sufficient to convince data processing managers. Perhaps that's because DP managers have been promised too many miracles already -- decision tables, virtual memory, data base, distributed systems, and goodness-knows-what-else. Perhaps it's because the common-sense sales pitch makes structured programming sound like just another brand of toothpaste or dog food -- and we've all grown a little cynical and skeptical about *that* kind of selling.

In any case, it's been my experience that the most convincing arguments have been based on *real* experiences -- in other words, *real* case studies in which people have used structured programming, chief programmer teams, librarians, walkthroughs, or some other aspect of the PPT techniques, *with documented results*. Fortunately, there are a growing number of such case studies in existence today: Almost every computer conference contains one or two such case studies; almost every issue of *Datamation*, *Infosystems*, *Computer Decisions*, or *Computerworld* contains some kind of "we tried it and it worked..." testimonial. You would be well advised to keep an eye on these and other popular computer journals, to build your own file of testimonials with which to convince skeptical members of your EDP department.

The only problem with the case studies is that they all measure their results differently. As we pointed out in our earlier discussion of productivity, some organizations *include* system testing and documentation in their productivity measures, while others do not; some organizations include analysts, managers, and clerical staff in their measurements, while others count only the programmers. Thus, it may be very difficult to compare the results of an organization which reported its results in last month's issue of *Datamation* with the results of another organization which reported its results at the last National Computer Conference.

There is, fortunately, one set of statistics that is based on a uniform set of measurements. That set of statistics comes from

IBM, and was reported by Mr. Bill Pattison at the 1975 IEEE COMPCON Conference in Washington, D.C. Mr. Pattison's statistics are based on a survey of 51 different programming projects carried out by IBM's Federal Systems Division -- all of which made use of some aspect of the PPT techniques.

As Table 2.1 indicates, the scope of projects included in the survey was enormous -- ranging from tiny 900-line programs to immense systems of 712,000 lines. In each of these projects, though, the same questions were asked of the project manager: "Did your project make significant use of the Chief Programmer Team concept? Did your project make significant use of Structured Coding?" ... and so forth.

The results are summarized in Table 2.2. It is clear from the figures that the most significant influence on a project is the customer: a friendly customer who knows what he wants, and who does not change his mind -- that is what the project manager would most like to have! Also, the experience and qualifications of the programming personnel seemed to have a significant impact on productivity -- confirming, in a somewhat less dramatic way, the results of the Sackman experiment.

In addition, the figures tell us that PPT techniques improve programmer productivity by a factor of 1.5 to 2.0. It is unfortunate that IBM did not include structured design as a distinct methodology in this study, though it may have been included as part of top-down development. In any case, other experiments have suggested that structured design, by itself, also has the effect of increasing productivity by a factor of 1.5 to 2.0.

It's also unfortunate that this study -- and most other studies like it -- did not comment on the increase in program reliability achieved with the PPT techniques. However, other IBM experiments (notably the New York Times system and the Skylab system), as well as projects conducted by other organizations, have indicated that the PPT techniques enable us to write programs with an average of one to five bugs per 10,000 statements ... that is, programs that are roughly 100 times more reliable than programs produced by classical techniques.

Finally, the IBM study -- and most similar studies did not provide any quantitative data on the increased maintainability of a system produced with the PPT techniques. Obviously, if the system is 100 times more reliable than it would have been with classical techniques, the maintenance effort will be reduced. But what about the ease of adding new features to the system? Thus far, virtually everyone who has used the PPT techniques has agreed that the resulting systems are *qualitatively* easier to maintain and modify, but I have not yet seen any organization reporting that their maintenance effort has been reduced from 50% of the overall budget to 37.54%. Since the PPT techniques are still relatively new, and since it takes a while for maintenance savings to be felt, we may have to wait a few years to see the kind of statistics we would like to see. Our experiences thus far suggest that maintenance will be improved by a factor of 2.0 to 10.0 as a result of the PPT techniques.

Table 2.1: Range of projects in IBM survey.

	Low	High	Median
Size of system (lines of code)	900	712,000	21,000
Manpower (man-months)	3	11,760	60
Duration of project (months)	1	68	10

Table 2.2: Effect of PPT techniques.

	Low*	High	Factor
Chief Programmer Team	219**	408	1.9
Structured Code	169	301	1.8
Top-Down Development	198	321	1.6
Code Reviews (Walkthroughs)	220	339	1.5
Customer Interface Complexity	500	124	-4.0
Personnel Qualification and Experience	132	410	3.1

*In this survey, "low" meant a "low response," or negative response, to a particular question. Thus, the "low" category for "chief programmer team" means that the project manager did not use the chief programmer team concept at all, or that he used it minimally.

**This figure represents the average productivity of those projects which gave a "low" response to a particular question. The productivity is expressed as "lines of delivered, debugged source code per man-month," a measure which included *all* of the people charged on the project, and *all* of the time (design time, coding time, test time, documentation time, etc.) charged on the project. Thus, that subset of the 51 projects which did *not* use the chief programmer team concept had an average productivity of 219 lines of delivered (i.e., actually given to the customer, as opposed to test code and support code which was ultimately thrown away), debugged source code per man-month; those projects which *did* use the chief programmer team project had an average productivity of 408 lines of delivered, debugged source code per man-month.

Chapter 3 HOW TO MANAGE TOP-DOWN DESIGN AND TESTING

In this chapter, we begin discussing the PPT techniques in depth. This chapter deals specifically with two related techniques: *top-down design* and *top-down testing*.

The format of the chapter is very simple: First, a brief overview of the technical concepts behind the top-down approach; second, a review of the management-oriented benefits of the top-down approach; third, a discussion of the problems and difficulties that you, as a manager, are likely to encounter when implementing the top-down approach in your organization.

3.1 An Overview of the Top-Down Approach

Top-down design and top-down testing have been practiced instinctively by many programmers for years and years. In academic circles, it has been discussed as "systematic programming," "stepwise refinement," "levels of abstraction," and a variety of other names. The descriptive phrase "top-down" seems to dominate the other buzz-words these days, though, and one can find a variety of books and articles dealing with the subject.

My purpose in this section is to provide you with enough of an understanding of these important concepts of design and implementation to enable you to discuss them intelligently with your technical people -- and with other EDP managers. I am *not* trying to make you an expert on top-down design, and I certainly don't intend to say everything there is to be said on the subject (even if I were capable of doing so!). If you and/or your programmers require a more detailed discussion of the top-down approach, the references at the end of this chapter should prove helpful.

Before discussing the top-down approach, I should warn you that many EDP people use the phrase "top-down" rather loosely. For reasons that are largely historical in nature, top-down design and structured programming have long been discussed together; indeed, you'll notice that many of the references at the end of this chapter have a title that emphasizes "structured programming," and often does not mention "top-down" at all. There is nothing wrong with the fact that people have long discussed and practiced top-down design and structured programming together. Just make sure that when *you* are discussing top-down design with one of your colleagues, *he* is not thinking about structured programming -- *that* will have to wait until Chapter 5!

Also, when you are discussing the top-down approach with a colleague, make sure that you're both discussing the same *aspect* of the top-down approach. We can identify three related, but distinct, aspects of "top-down":

- top-down *design*, which can be described as a design strategy that breaks large, complex problems into smaller, less complex problems -- and then decomposes each of those smaller problems into even smaller problems, until the original problem has been expressed as some combination of many small, *solvable* problems.

- top-down *coding*, which can be described as a strategy of *coding* high-level (e.g., "executive") modules as soon as they have been designed -- and generally before the low-level "detail" modules have been designed.

- top-down *testing*, or top-down *implementation*, which can be described as a strategy of testing the high-level modules of a system before the low-level modules have been coded -- and possibly before they have been designed.

What a perfectly simple idea! Indeed, what more does one have to say by way of an introduction to the top-down approach? Well, perhaps a simple example would be useful to illustrate top-down design *and* top-down coding *and* top-down testing. Consider that most universal of all commercial data processing systems, the payroll system.

I had the opportunity a few years ago to participate in a payroll project in which we began by breaking the entire system into an edit, an update, a sort, and several print routines. ("What's so special about that?" you say to yourself. "We've been doing that sort of thing for years!" Of course! That's just the point: Many organizations have followed some form of top-down design all along.) Having identified these top-level "modules" and the next few levels of modules beneath them, we wrote code for the top-level modules -- in many cases, we wrote code to call lower-level modules that we had not yet designed.

The primary purpose of this coding exercise was to make it possible to test -- or "exercise," as we preferred to call it, since the testing was not exhaustive -- a preliminary version of the payroll system -- a payroll system that was, in a sense, a *complete* payroll system. Approximately three weeks after beginning the project, we produced what was referred to as "version 1": a payroll system that accepted input transactions and a master file, and which produced paychecks.

Of course, our version 1 payroll system had a few minor limitations. The user was required to provide error-free transactions, for our payroll system made no attempt to validate them. In addition, the user was required to provide transactions that had already been sorted, as our system was too lazy to do the sorting. Furthermore, our system was unwilling to allow the user to hire new employees, fire existing employees, give any employees a salary increase -- or, for that matter, make *any* change to an employee's current status.

To add insult to injury, our payroll system uniformly paid everyone a salary of $100 per week, and withheld a uniform $15 in taxes from everyone's paycheck. It insisted that all employees be paid by check (instead of allowing the convenience of being paid by cash, or having one's paycheck deposited directly into a bank account). The final indignity: It printed all of the paychecks in octal.

Not a very exciting payroll system! On the other hand, it *did* involve all of the top-level modules. What made the system so primitive was the fact that all of the lower-level modules existed as "stubs," or "dummy routines." For example, the top-level module in the update portion of the system called a module to compute an employee's salary; for the version 1 system, that module simply returned an output of $100. Similarly, the top-level module in the edit part of the system called a module to determine the validity of a specific transaction; for version 1, that module simply returned with an indication that the transaction was valid -- without going to any effort to *actually* validate the transaction.

Subsequent versions of the payroll system merely involved adding lower-level modules to the existing skeleton of top-level modules. A second version of the system, for example, allowed the user to hire and fire employees; it also sorted the transactions; and, in a few very simple cases, it actually computed an employee's gross pay. However, version 2 still made no attempt to validate the input transactions. In most cases, it still paid employees $100 per week; and in all cases, it withheld $15 in taxes; and in all cases, it still printed paychecks in octal. Subsequent versions added in these details, until a final version produced output that was satisfactory to the user.

That, in a nutshell, is the top-down approach. The concept of top-down *design* is very simple, and has been around for a long time. Indeed, one could argue that it is just a variation of Julius Caesar's "divide and conquer" strategy. Most intelligent programmers would argue that they've been doing top-down design all along; and most serious data processing managers would argue that they have always enforced top-down design in their department.

However, my visits to several hundred organizations around the world during the past ten years suggest otherwise: Many managers promote good design strategies in their standards manuals but fail to enforce them; many programmers follow such a sloppy and informal version of top-down design that they are unable to take advantage of its benefits. Some programmers attempt to practice "bottom-up" design (that is, they first try to identify all of the bottom-level modules that will be required, and then try to figure out how to put them together). Finally, the majority of programmers do *no* design, but rather begin coding as soon as they have been given specifications.

Still, it is probably fair to say that many organizations attempt to practice top-down design. By contrast, very *few* organizations make any conscious attempt at top-down testing. The few organizations that have some kind of formal test plan advocate a "bottom-up" strategy. First, the bottom-level modules are tested in isolation. Then, the bottom-level modules are combined with modules at the next higher level to form programs, which are tested in isolation. Next, the programs are combined with modules at the next higher level to form subsystems, which are tested in isolation. Finally, all of the subsystems are combined to permit a "system test."

So, if your programmers tell you that they are already doing top-down design and top-down testing, beware! Look more closely at what they are *really* doing: Could they really give you, for example, a payroll system that paid all employees $100 in octal shortly after the beginning of the project?

3.2 The Benefits of the Top-Down Approach

The benefits of top-down design should be immediately obvious. Most problems (whether in the data processing field or anywhere else) are too complex to be grasped in their entirety. Top-down design provides an organized method of breaking the original problem into smaller problems that we *can* grasp, and that we *can* solve with some degree of success.

The benefits of top-down testing are not so immediately apparent -- particularly in organizations that have followed the bottom-up approach for the past ten or twenty years. Those benefits are summarized in the following sections.

3.2.1 Major interfaces are exercised at the beginning of the project

In the brief sketch painted earlier of the payroll system, version 1 demonstrated that the edit subsystem could communicate -- to some limited extent -- with the update subsystem, which in turn was capable of communicating with the sort subsystem, which in turn was capable of communicating with the various print routines.

In any major computer system, one can usually identify subsystems, *and interfaces between the subsystems.* Those interfaces may be implemented in the form of a magnetic tape file, or a disk file, or data passed from module to module through core memory. Typically, the interface will be documented by the designer(s) on paper: some documentation of the file layout, the intermodule calling sequence, or something of that nature. Unfortunately, individual programmers may interpret the interface documents slightly differently; they may code bugs into that portion of their program that passes information through the interface; the interface document may be blatantly incorrect (a common occurrence with certain information supplied by computer vendors!); or the interface document may be incomplete, failing to describe certain conditions, exceptions, or special situations.

What we are saying, then, is that the interface between modules, and the interface between subsystems, is a common place for bugs to occur. In the bottom-up approach, *major* interfaces are usually not tested until the very end -- at which point, the discovery of an interface bug can be disastrous! The presence of the interface bug may require that several modules be recoded; even worse, it often occurs the day before the final deadline -- or the day *after* the final deadline!

By contrast, the top-down approach tends to *force* important, top-level interfaces to be exercised at an early stage in the project, so that if there are problems, they can be resolved while there is still the time, the energy, and the resources to deal with them. Indeed, we usually find that as we go further and further in the project, the bugs become simpler and simpler -- that is, the interface problems become more and more localized.

We should emphasize that the term "interface problems" includes not only the interfaces between major pieces of an application system, but also the interfaces between the vendor's hardware and your applications, as well as the interfaces between the vendor's systems software and your applications. Thus, one of my clients found that version 1 of their on-line system represented a major test of a CRT terminal (with which they had had no prior experience); a new modem; newly installed telephone lines; a newly acquired telecommunications monitor from a major software firm; a newly acquired data base management system from a different software firm; the vendor's operating system; *and* several major application subsystems.

You can imagine the sort of things that were discovered in version 1: The vendor's terminal worked, but the programming manual for the terminal left out some key details that would have caused major problems if they had not been discovered at an early stage. The modem had the nasty habit of dropping bits of data at random intervals. The telephone lines actually worked, to everyone's surprise(!) but the telecommunications monitor "gobbled up" all available memory in the computer, fragmented the memory into small pieces, and then shut down the system because it could not obtain enough "big" chunks of memory. The data base management package worked fine, but could only carry out one disk access at a time, a fact which would have caused major throughput problems if it had not been discovered at an early stage. All of the application subsystems had a variety of interface bugs. It was a wonder the client ever got version 1 working at all -- but when they did, it was relatively smooth sailing from there on!

3.2.2 Users can see a working demonstration of the system

Perhaps the single most important advantage of the top-down approach is that one can demonstrate a skeleton version of a system to a user at an early stage -- *before* the programmers have wasted a great deal of time coding from fuzzy, inaccurate specifications.

This point brings up one of the most serious philosophical problems in the computer field today: what I like to call the "myth of perfect systems analysis." There is a feeling that *if* one spends enough time talking to the user or *if* one puts a user on the design team; or, conversely, *if* one makes the programmers work *in* the user department; or *if* one gets the user to formally sign and accept the specification; and *if* a few other well-intentioned gimmicks are implemented, -- then it will be possible to get perfect specifications, from which we can write perfect code that will make the user perfectly happy.

Humbug! There may be a few cases where this has worked to some degree, but it is largely an exercise in futility. First, in any new, sophisticated computer system, the user does *not* know what he wants -- and he *won't* know what he wants until he begins to see, in terms of something more tangible than a stack of flowcharts and narrative descriptions, what he can get.

Second, one must recognize that communication problems between the user, the analyst, and the programmer are inevitable. The user will explain what he wants in a language that is incomplete, ambiguous, and imprecise. The analyst and the programmer will misinterpret the user's wishes in a variety of subtle ways -- not to mention the simple human errors they are likely to make.

Finally, one must accept that, in today's world, things often change more quickly than we can develop computer systems. I have seen a number of systems that were specified in 1970-71, and were scheduled to be installed in 1975. By 1975, most of the major premises upon which the systems were based had changed: The business had changed, the economy had changed, the technology had changed, the competition had changed. Indeed, even the user had changed -- the "ultimate system" was delivered to a person other than the one who originally ordered it.

All of these phenomena -- of which you should be painfully aware in your own organization -- argue strongly for a top-down approach. Even if the user seems to know what he wants, implement a top-level skeleton first -- and make him look at it! Chances are, he'll want something deleted from the original specifications or something added. In general, it is easier to make changes *before* coding. In many cases, one can avoid the frustrating experience of writing a beautiful set of code, only to throw it away because the user changed his mind!

3.2.3 Deadline problems can be dealt with in a more satisfactory manner

Though this book is aimed at managers, and is concerned with problems of management, it is not a book on "project management." I say this because, with all of our experience, projects are *still* typically behind schedule and over budget.

Why? Partly, I suspect, because deadlines reflect political pressures more than they reflect the sober, rational judgment of a manager. The reason the deadline is January 1st is because someone insisted that the system must be operational for the beginning of the new fiscal year -- and to hell with your PERT charts!

The other major reason for deadline problems is the occurrence of unforeseen events. If all of the programmers come down with the bubonic plague, the project will probably be late; if a tornado demolishes the computer room, things will probably fall behind schedule.

All of this is well known. And yet many of us persist in drawing neater, and more accurate PERT charts -- in the hopes that users and top management someday will allow us to schedule our projects on a rational basis. And many of us continue assuming that there will be no tornadoes and no outbursts of bubonic plague -- and that users and top management will someday be sympathetic to the problems of meeting a deadline with handicaps like those.

The point of all this is that when the deadline arrives, the classical bottom-up approach usually leaves us in a vulnerable position. Typically, we find that the design has been completed, most (or all) of the code has been written, and most (possibly all) of the modules have been tested individually. Unfortunately, when the modules are assembled together, they *don't* work. That is, when the deadline arrives, we find that we are in the middle of system testing -- with 20,000 lines of code that don't *do* anything. Try to explain that to a user who doesn't know the difference between a line of code and a football.

And try to explain it to top managers who have been getting status reports all along indicating that things are on schedule! Chances are, you've been fooled, too. Your programmers probably began telling you on the second day of the project that they were 95% done -- and on "deadline day," they are *still* 95% done! Sure, they reached the milestone of "design completed" on schedule -- but what does that mean? And they reached the milestone of "all modules coded" on schedule -- but what does that mean?

Compare that with the top-down approach. Recognize first that there is no magic in this world: Whether one works top-down or bottom-up, there will *still* be deadline problems. The system will *still* be unfinished when the deadline arrives, and the users will *still* be irritated (even if you never agreed to the deadline!).

However, you will probably be in a much stronger political position than you would be with the bottom-up approach -- because you will have a skeleton version of the system that performs some demonstrable processing. Of course, this has to be taken with a small grain of salt: If we are still working with a payroll system that produces octal paychecks, the user might well send us off to the slave labor camps in Siberia. However, one can imagine the following kind of dialogue:

User: "Good morning. Today's the deadline.... Where is my payroll system?"

DP Manager: "I'm sorry to say that we're not finished."

User: "What!? That's ridiculous!! We agreed that you would be finished by January 1st!"

DP Manager: "Actually, *you* agreed that it would be done on January 1st -- I told you all along that that date was optimistic. However, I do have a version 3 payroll system that works and can be put into operation today."

User: "Version 3? What's that mean?"

DP Manager: "Well, that's a payroll system that pays everyone by check; it won't pay anyone in cash, or by direct bank deposit. And if anyone works double overtime, the system will pay them $100 per week. And the system does not validate transactions that *decrease* an employee's salary, which means that an employee's salary might accidentally be reduced below zero. But, other than those minor details, the system works just fine."

User: "That's ridiculous!! That's unacceptable!! I want the whole thing!! I asked for the whole payroll system to be working by January 1st!!"

DP Manager: "I know -- but we didn't make it. In the meantime, you should be able to live with these minor restrictions. We'll have them fixed in another two weeks."

User: "Grumble, grumble ... well, I suppose it's better than nothing."

3.2.4 Debugging is easier

One of the advantages of the top-down approach is a *technical* matter that shouldn't concern you as a manager; nevertheless, it can't hurt you to be aware of it.

To explain this point, we need to draw the distinction between *testing* and *debugging*. Loosely speaking, *testing* is the process one goes through to demonstrate the correctness (or incorrectness) of a program or system; it usually consists of supplying known inputs to the system and verifying that the outputs are correct. *Debugging*, on the other hand, is the black art of tracking down a bug once its existence has been made known. The existence of a bug is usually learned from a controlled test procedure -- which is why testing and debugging are considered almost synonymous by most programmers. But when a production program blows up in the middle of the night, and the computer operator calls up the responsible programmer -- it's *debugging* that the poor, sleepy programmer is doing, not testing!

Given that distinction, we argue that *debugging* tends to be easier in a top-down testing environment than in a bottom-up testing environment. Why? Because top-down testing tends to be *incremental* in nature. That is, it usually consists of adding one new module to an existing skeleton of modules, and then observing the behavior of the new system. If the new system misbehaves, common sense tells the programmer that the problem is probably located in the new module -- or in the interface between the new module and the rest of the system. Indeed, if the programmer gets desperate, he always has the option of "strategic retreat": He can remove the new module, re-insert the dummy, or "stub," in its place, and retreat to his office to contemplate the mystery of the bug.

By contrast, the bottom-up approach tends to be "phased" in nature. That is, one usually finds geometrically increasing numbers of modules being combined together for the first time -- any one of which (or any combination of which) may contain a bug. This is particularly evident during system testing, when hundreds (or even thousands) of modules are combined together for the first time -- and one of those modules contains a bug which ultimately destroys the entire system. Even worse, a bug in module A combines with a bug in module B to produce a subtly incorrect output that the programmer finds impossible to relate to any single module; or a bug in module A cancels the effect of a bug in module B, thus leading to correct output -- until the maintenance programmer innocently fixes the bug in module A!

3.2.5 Requirements for machine test time are distributed more evenly throughout a top-down project

It has been observed in many projects that the requirement for machine time rises almost exponentially toward the end of the project. By contrast, the requirement for machine time in a top-down project remains fairly constant during the lifetime of the project.

The differences between the two approaches can be shown graphically as follows:

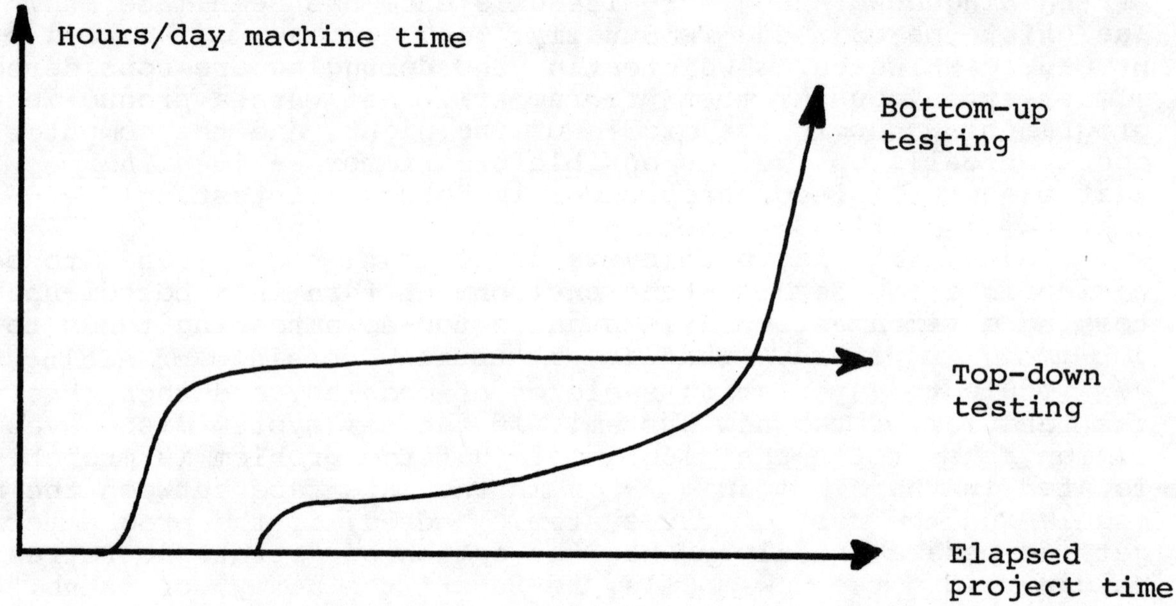

You should be able to anticipate the reasons for these two curves from what we have already said about the top-down approach. The bottom-up approach generally does not begin using computer test time until the project is well underway -- simply because the approach involves designing and coding all (or most) of the system before any testing begins. Once testing begins, the requirement for machine time rises rapidly as modules are combined into programs, programs into subsystems, and subsystems into systems.

By contrast, the top-down approach begins using machine time earlier. This is possible because one begins writing code before the design is finished. Normally, we find that the requirement for test time reaches a certain point, and then levels off -- remaining relatively constant for the duration of the project. The reason for the constant requirement for test time is fairly simple: The incremental nature of the testing involves adding one new module to the system each day, and running roughly the same set of test data through the system. It should be noted that early use of machine time can cause some problems, which are discussed in Section 3.3.2.

3.2.6 Programmer morale is improved

A minor advantage of the top-down approach -- but one which should not be ignored -- is the fact that the programmers are usually happier and better motivated. Why? For the same reasons that users and managers like the top-down approach: They can see tangible results of progress at an earlier stage.

This may be a significant point. Programmers, for the most part, *do* like to program. They do *not* like to write detailed specifications, they do *not* like to write flowcharts, they do *not* like to become engrossed in the paperwork that is characteristic of the early stages of a typical project. Not being terribly enthusiastic about such work, they tend to work 9-to-5 days -- at best! When they get into the programming and testing -- the *fun* part -- *then* they begin to work the 16-hour days that we come to depend on.

With the top-down approach, the programming usually begins much earlier in the project -- which means that the programmer can begin doing, at an earlier stage, that which he really enjoys. On top of this, he has the tremendous morale boost of seeing a version 1 system actually work. It doesn't matter that the version 1 payroll system is trivial and that it only produces octal pay-checks -- it is a *real* program that accepts *real* inputs and produces *real* outputs! That alone is probably sufficient to motivate the programmer to work 16-hour days to produce version 2 of the system.

3.2.7 Top-down testing eliminates the need for test harnesses

Finally, we mention a characteristic of top-down testing that is basically technical in nature, although it has some management overtones.

We observe that the classic bottom-up scheme usually requires the presence of a "test driver," or "test harness" -- that is, a program which can read in test data from a file, pass the test data to the module being tested, capture the output from the module, and print the output on a suitable output device. A few organizations are disciplined enough to require their programmers to make use of a "general-purpose" test driver (along with a general-purpose test data generator, perhaps), but most organizations don't bother. That is, in most companies, each programmer writes a "quick-and-dirty" test driver for each of the modules he is testing.

By contrast, the top-down approach eliminates the need for drivers -- since the existing skeleton system can serve as a natural test driver for a new detail module being added to the system.

On the other hand, the top-down approach *does* require the use of "stubs," or "dummy routines." Such routines substitute for detailed modules that have not yet been coded, and their implementation usually consists of:

1. Immediate exit, with no processing

2. Returning constant output -- e.g., returning $100 in the "dummy" version of the salary computation module in the payroll system mentioned above

3. Returning a "random" number within some range

4. Printing an output message, to inform the programmer that the dummy module was executed

5. Executing a timing loop to consume N micro-seconds in a controlled fashion (useful in some real-time systems)

6. Providing a primitive "quick-and-dirty" implementation of the *real* function of the module.

Though I see nothing fundamentally wrong with test drivers, it is worth observing that dummy routines are usually simpler to code than a corresponding driver routine. In the best case, the dummy routine consists of one statement: EXIT.

3.3 Management Problems with the Top-Down Approach

Based on the preceding discussion, you might be tempted to issue a memo to your programmers -- one which says: "Troops! starting tomorrow, I want all of you to design and test your systems in a top-down fashion!" Or maybe you should send all 300 of your programmers to a one-hour class on top-down implementation, and *then* issue the edict....

As you recall from Chapter 2, I suggested that an approach like this is likely to lead to a certain degree of chaos and confusion. Indeed, even if you ease into top-down implementation slowly and gradually (and diplomatically), you may experience a certain degree of chaos and confusion. The troops, even with the best of intentions, are likely to do some silly things in the name of top-down implementation.

What sort of things? Well, it varies from company to company -- but the sort of problems that I have seen are as follows:

1. A misunderstanding of "radical" top-down implementation versus "conservative" top-down implementation

2. Lack of sufficient test time

3. Lack of hardware for top-down testing

4. Staffing problems

5. Programmers' fear that changes to low-level modules will propagate up to high-level modules

6. Common tendency to practice top-down *program* testing, combined with bottom-up *system* testing

7. Discipline problems in multi-team projects

8. Difficulty visualizing top-down versions.

Each of these potential problem areas requires a brief discussion.

3.3.1 The misunderstanding between "radical" top-down and "conservative" top-down

At this point, you may well be wondering, "What's 'conservative' top-down? What's 'radical' top-down? Where was that discussed?" Indeed, it was *not* discussed -- and *because* it's not discussed, many organizations get into trouble when they first attempt the top-down approach.

We could describe the "radical" top-down approach in the following manner: First, design the top level of a system -- e.g., recognize that the payroll system mentioned earlier will have a top-level edit module, a top-level update module, and a variety of top-level print modules. Having done this much design, *immediately* write the code for those modules, and test them as a version 1 system. Next, design the second-level modules -- i.e., the modules at the next level below the top-level modules just completed. Having designed the second-level modules, next write the code and test a version 2 system. And so forth...

The "conservative" approach to top-down implementation, on the other hand, goes something like this: Design all of the top-level modules. Then, design all of the modules at the second level; then, all of the modules at the third level; and so forth, until the entire design is finished. At that point, write the code for the top-level modules, and implement them as a version 1 system. From the experience gained in implementing the version 1 system, make any necessary changes to the lower levels of design; then code and test the modules at the second level. And so forth...

The important thing to realize is that the "radical" approach and the "conservative" approach represent the two extreme points on a spectrum; there are an infinite number of "compromise" top-down strategies that you can select, depending on your situation. You may decide, for example, to finish 75% of the design -- and then begin coding and testing those modules that you have designed (obviously, the coding and testing would be done top-down). Or you might decide to design 25% of the system -- and then, with 75% of the system still quite "fuzzy," start coding and implementing.

As you might have guessed, there is no single "right" answer. I cannot tell you whether the "radical" approach is better than the "conservative" approach for all possible projects. However, I *can* identify the primary factors that will help *you* decide just how radical or conservative you will want to be:

1. *User "fickleness."* If the user has no idea of what he wants, or is prone to changing his mind, I would opt for the radical approach. Why waste time designing a great deal of detailed logic that will be thrown away? On the other hand, if the user knows precisely what he wants, I might attempt a complete design.

2. *Quality of the design.* Committing oneself to code too early in the project may make it difficult to "improve" the design later on. All other things being equal, we would prefer to finish the entire design; we will discuss this further in Section 3.3.5 below.

3. *Time pressures.* If you are under extreme pressure from users or higher levels of management to produce some tangible output quickly, go for the radical approach. If your deadline is absolutely inflexible -- i.e., if it is a case of "you bet your job" -- go for the radical approach. If you are not under much pressure, and if the deadline is flexible, go for the conservative approach.

4. *Accurate estimates.* If you are required by your organization to provide accurate, detailed estimates of schedules, manpower, and other resources, then you should opt for the conservative approach. How can you estimate how long it will take to implement the system until you know how many modules it will contain?

All of this makes sense -- at least, it *should* make sense. The reason that problems have occurred in this area is primarily because the top-down approach has been interpreted by some programmers and managers and users as a kind of religion -- but all three parties tend to interpret that religion differently.

To the user community, "top-down" means that they should have a working system on the second day of the project -- and it should be a perfect design! And the programmers sometimes interpret the religion as an official license to begin writing code on the second day of the project -- which unfortunately degenerates into coding without *any* design!

In practice, hardly anyone follows the extreme "radical" approach described earlier. Most designers instinctively explore at least half of the design before committing themselves to code -- even if much of that design is subconscious and undocumented! Unfortunately, many projects *do* seem to follow the extreme "conservative" approach -- and while it may, in general, lead to better technical designs, it fails for two reasons: (a) on a large project, the user is incapable of specifying the details with any accuracy, and (b) on a large project, users and top management are increasingly unwilling to accept two or three years of effort by the EDP department with no visible, tangible output. Hence, the movement toward the "radical" approach.

The important thing for you, as a manager, is: Don't let the users bamboozle you into a radical approach in situations where that seems inappropriate. Don't let your project management textbooks bamboozle you into following the "conservative" approach of developing the perfect design when you know, in the pit of your stomach, that the user is really uncertain about what he wants. And finally, don't let the programmers bamboozle you into thinking that top-down implementation means that they are automatically free to begin writing code on the first day of the project.

3.3.2 Lack of sufficient machine time

In several of the organizations I have visited, the programmers complain to me (sometimes privately, so that the boss won't get irritated) that they get only one test shot a day -- in other words, they have to wait 24 hours to see the output of any test run that they have submitted. In a few organizations, the programmers may get as little as one test shot a week.

In addition, the programmers will sometimes complain that they can't get *any* machine time when they need it. As we observed in an earlier section, the top-down approach requires machine availability at an earlier point in time during the project life cycle -- and this may cause problems in organizations which always assumed that the programmers wouldn't need any machine time until the project was six months underway.

In most of the organizations where this problem has come up, the programmers have abandoned top-down testing partially or completely -- often without even knowing it. Instead of adding only *one* new module to an existing skeleton and testing the system incrementally, the programmers begin adding *all* of the modules at a particular level (e.g., all of the second-level edit modules in the payroll system) and testing them en masse. In the worst case, the programmers will retreat to the bottom-up approach with which they are more familiar.

So, my advice to you is to ensure that your programmers have enough machine time to indulge in the top-down approach -- at least for their first few projects, when they occasionally may be tempted to slip back into their old ways.

How *much* machine time should you allocate? Should one expect to use more machine time with the top-down approach than would have been used with the bottom-up approach? The honest answer, at this stage in our experience with the PPT techniques, is: We don't know. You will probably be safe if you allocate roughly as much test time as you would have allocated with your classical bottom-up techniques; and then use the experience of your first few "pilot projects" (a concept discussed in more detail in Chapter 11) to refine your estimates.

My experience has been that the *amount* of machine time is somewhat less important than the *frequency* of test shots. If the programmer knows that he is going to have only one test shot a week, it is almost impossible to resist the temptation to throw *all* of his modules into the machine at once and hope that they'll all work. On the other hand, if he knows that he'll get two or three test shots a day, he will be more inclined to follow the incremental approach of testing one new module at a time.

By the way, one reason for my inability to predict the amount of machine time that you will need in a top-down project is that very few projects (indeed, *none* that I have worked on) use *only* top-down implementation. Most organizations use top-down implementation, *plus* structured design, *plus* structured walkthroughs, *plus* ... The overall result, generally, is much *less* machine time. If your programmers write code with no bugs, then they will need a modest amount of machine time to *verify* that they have no bugs -- but, *they will need no debugging time*, and *they will need no computer time for re-compiling and re-testing their programs*.

3.3.3 Lack of hardware for testing

Not getting *enough* machine time for testing is one problem; not getting *any* machine time for testing is a qualitatively different problem. The most extreme form of this phenomenon occurs in projects that have *no* computer hardware during the system development phase.

Many of today's on-line systems run into this problem. In order to carry out top-down implementation, the programmers require access to terminals, modems, multiplexors, and communication lines -- in addition to the conventional "central site" hardware. If this is the organization's *first* on-line system, the terminals and communication equipment may not exist -- *and management is frequently reluctant to install the communication equipment until the last possible moment.*

The result? Bottom-up development, in one form or another. A great deal of application software will be written and tested in a batch environment, or, at best, in a "simulated" on-line environment -- and an attempt will be made, sometimes on the day before the deadline, to interface all of this software with the newly arrived teleprocessing hardware/software.

The reason for management's reluctance is obvious: The teleprocessing equipment is expensive, and management is concerned that it will be idle for a substantial portion of the development phase of the project. On the other hand, my experience has been that the equipment will be idle *anyway*, while the programmers try to find their bugs -- the only question is whether you would prefer to have the equipment installed and idle *before* the deadline, or *after* the deadline.

Obviously, compromises can be made in this area. If an on-line system will eventually have 1,000 terminals, we could expect to carry out a reasonable form of top-down implementation with three or four terminals and one or two communication lines. If certain pieces of hardware are simply *not* available (perhaps because they haven't been built), then "simulator" software is better than nothing.

3.3.4 Staffing problems

In some organizations, a full complement of programmers, analysts, and designers is assigned to a programming project *on the first day of the project*. Sometimes this is the result of contractual and billing procedures -- particularly in dealings between a software/consulting organization and a separate user organization.

Sometimes, though, the problem is much more mundane. As a manager, you know that you'll need Fred and Susy in the middle of the project. Unfortunately, if you don't grab them now -- at the beginning of the project -- they'll be occupied with something else when you need them. Rather than lose them, you may decide to bring them into your project -- even though there is nothing for them to do.

The result of this kind of management decision should be obvious. In an attempt to keep Fred and Susy busy, someone will "invent" some bottom-level modules *that they hope will be needed later on.* Fred and Susy will then be sent off to code these modules -- and the rest of the team continues to work on the *top* part of the system.

Of course, the problem is that subsequent design work may show that nobody really needs Fred's module after all -- and that the interface that was specified for Susy's module is completely impractical. That's the risk one runs when combining top-down design with bottom-up design!

Two things should be observed here. First, it is often practical to have several programmer/analysts working on the top portion of the system -- even if they function only as coders, reviewers (i.e., indulging in the structured walkthrough concept discussed in Chapter 9), or librarians (i.e., indulging in the concept explored in Chapter 8). Thus, Fred and Susy might be very useful as participants in the top-level design -- *more* useful, perhaps, than sending them off to code bottom-level modules that may never be needed.

Second, it is a good idea to complete all, or most, of the design of the system before trying to figure out how many Freds and Susys will be required to code the individual module. Thus, the normal problems of staffing and resource planning are often a strong argument for the "conservative" top-down approach.

3.3.5 Programmers' fear that changes to low-level modules will propagate up to the top-level modules

It might not have occurred to you that programmers sometimes object to the top-down approach. Relatively few do object, but those who do, frequently mention one major concern: The implementation of bottom-level modules, late in the project, may cause problems in top-level modules that have already been designed, coded, and tested.

In my experience, this concern is usually exaggerated. Yes, the implementation of bottom-level modules may suggest or even require changes to some of the higher-level modules, but this is usually fairly minor. It is *possible* that the implementation of the last bottom-level module will uncover design flaws that will propagate throughout the rest of the system ... but it's rather unlikely.

If it appears that this may be a serious problem on your project -- or something that is going to bother your programmers -- then you should opt for the "conservative" top-down approach. Finish the entire design before writing any code. That way, you'll be able to anticipate almost all of the potential design problems with bottom-level modules.

At the same time, note that this problem is identical to the one frequently observed in a bottom-up project. At the very end of the pilot, when two major subsystems are linked together for the first time, we find that the interface isn't right -- subsystem A is passing the wrong kind of data to subsystem B (usually because someone misread or misunderstood the interface documentation). Correcting that problem -- a problem discovered late in the project life cycle, at the top of the system structure -- may propagate all the way down to the bottom-level modules. My experience has been that problems of this sort are usually *much* worse than the problems discovered in the top-down approach.

Also, keep in mind that many of the problems will come from the user -- and this is an argument for using a more radical top-down implementation. There is no point in finishing the entire design and letting the programmers reassure themselves that all of the interfaces are proper, and that the design is perfect -- only to have half of it thrown out because the user changed his mind.

3.3.6 The mistake of top-down program testing and bottom-up system testing

This problem is characterized by the following kind of dialogue at the beginning of a project:

Boss: "OK, troops, let's break the system down into a bunch of individual programs."

Troops: "Right, boss."

Boss: "OK, Fred, you take program #1. Susy, you take program #2. Charlie, you take program #3. And I want all of you to use top-down testing, structured programming, and all of that stuff."

Troops: "Right, boss."

Boss: "And when you're all done, let's all get back together -- and then we'll put the programs together into a system."

As one might expect, this approach has many of the same problems as the original bottom-up approach. Fred, Susy, and Charlie find that their individual programming projects are quite easy -- the problems occur when they get back together again. At that point, they find that Fred decided to change the interface specifications without telling anyone; Susy's program doesn't work with Charlie's program; and so forth.

In most cases, this problem is the result of a misunderstanding of the top-down concept. Sometimes, it is the conscious result of other problems, such as lack of sufficient computer time.

Depending on the size of the project, this combination of top-down program development and bottom-up system development may or may not be serious. If Fred, Susy, and Charlie are writing small programs that require only a day's effort, then their "systems integration" difficulties should be manageable. But if this situation occurs with 50 programmers who spend a year developing their individual programs, chaos will probably reign supreme.

3.3.7 Discipline problems in multi-team projects

On very large projects, the programming group is usually broken into smaller "teams" -- each team being responsible for a program, or a subsystem, or some other measure of work. At that point, Mealy's Law* takes over: The eventual structure of the system reflects the structure of the organization that builds the system. If two teams have difficulty communicating with each other (because of personality problems or political problems), then their subsystems will probably have difficulty communicating with each other.

In particular, I have found that each team has a tendency to isolate itself from other teams. Early integration of the top-level skeleton of one team's subsystem with the top-level skeleton of another team's subsystem is often regarded as a hassle -- and both teams will avoid it. As a result, there is a tendency to use the approach discussed in the previous section: top-down program development and bottom-up systems integration.

Why is it a hassle interfacing two subsystems at an early stage? Because the interfaces are fuzzy! Team A hasn't really defined precisely what data they require from Team B -- and as a result, it's very difficult to put their two subsystems into the machine and make them communicate. But that is *precisely* what the top-down approach is trying to accomplish: *forcing* the precise definition of major interfaces, and forcing those interfaces to be coded and exercised in a computer to ensure that they work!

In other words, you should *expect* problems in this area -- the larger your project, the more problems there will be. Rather than avoiding the problems, you should confront them directly. That's what the top-down approach is all about.

3.3.8 Difficulty visualizing top-down "versions"

This is perhaps the most common problem -- and certainly the most serious. Many people -- particularly programmers -- seem to have a very confused notion of the sequence of implementation in a top-down project.

---

*So named after George Mealy, one of the architects of IBM's OS/360.

In our example of a payroll system, many programmers seem to think that top-down implementation means the following: Version 1 of the system will do all of the editing, but nothing else; version 2 of the system will combine all of the editing and all of the update logic (and thus all of the salary computations, tax calculations, etc.); version 3 will combine all of the editing, all of the update logic, and the sorting; and version 4 will throw in the printing.

I don't know why some programmers have had such difficulty visualizing a skeleton version of a *complete* system -- e.g., visualizing a payroll system that incorporates the top-level logic of the edit *and* the update *and* the printing. I can only warn you that it is likely to be a problem -- so watch out for it!

Chapter 3: References

1. Baker, F.T., "Chief Programmer Team Management of Production Programming," *IBM Systems Journal*, January 1972, pages 56-73. This classic article on the so-called New York Times system gives an illustration of top-down design as well as several other important PPT techniques discussed later in this book.

2. Dahl, O.J., E.W. Dijkstra, and C.A.R. Hoare, *Structured Programming*, Prentice-Hall, 1972. Another formal, scholarly view of top-down design.

3. Dijkstra, E., "Structured Programming," *Software Engineering*, NATO Scientific Affairs Division, Brussels 39, Belgium, 1969. Also republished recently as *Software Engineering Concepts and Techniques*, J.M. Buxton, Peter Naur, and Brian Randell (Editors), Petrocelli/Charter Publishers, 1976. Dijkstra's discussion is one of the first that refers to "top-down design" as "levels of abstraction."

4. McGowan, C.L., and J.R. Kelly, *Top-Down Structured Programming*, Petrocelli/Charter, 1975. A discussion of structured programming and top-down design, discussed primarily in terms of PL/I.

5. Mills, H.D., "Top-Down Programming in Large Systems," from *Debugging Techniques in Large Systems*, Prentice-Hall, 1971. Mills is one of IBM's foremost advocates of top-down design, top-down implementation, and other related PPT techniques.

6. Wirth, N., *Systematic Programming*, Prentice-Hall, 1973. A more theoretical and academic view of the "stepwise refinement" (Wirth's phrase for top-down design) process by one of the leading computer science scholars in the world.

7. Yourdon, E., *Techniques of Program Structure and Design*, Prentice-Hall, 1975. Chapter 2 of this book discusses the top-down approach, in terms meant to be understood by programmers, designers, and analysts.

8. Yourdon, Edward and Larry Constantine, *Structured Design*, YOURDON inc., 1975. Chapter 12 of this book discusses some of the weaknesses of the top-down approach, as it is normally practiced.

Chapter 4 HOW TO MANAGE STRUCTURED DESIGN

Having discussed top-down design, we turn now to a related topic: *structured design*. As in the previous chapter, we will begin with a brief overview of the technical concepts of structured design. This will be followed by a discussion of the problems you are likely to have in your attempt to implement structured design in your organization.

4.1 An Overview of Structured Design

The term "structured design" was introduced by IBM in an article in the *IBM Systems Journal* in 1974. Prior to that, many of the concepts that we will discuss in this chapter were known simply as "modular design," or "logical design," or "composite design," or "the design of program structure."

That last phrase says it all: We are concerned with the architecture, the organization, and the *structure* of computer programs -- and systems of programs. It is an area that people have talked about for years, but have only formalized in the past two or three years. The references at the end of this chapter contain most of the major writing on the subject -- and it will be noted that all of them have been published in the period since 1974.

We should begin our overview of structured design by observing that it is *not* the same as top-down design. Top-down design can be viewed as a strategy: Given a large, complex problem, what strategy is appropriate for solving it? One reasonable answer is: top-down design -- which is generally preferable to bottom-up design, random design, or no design.

On the other hand, top-down design -- as it is generally understood and practiced -- does *not* guarantee that we end up with a *good* design. To put it more bluntly, it is quite easy to design a *terrible* system in a top-down fashion. A "good" system, in the context of this discussion is one that is easy to implement, easy to debug, and easy to maintain; a "terrible" system is one that, for one reason or another, turns out to be expensive to develop and maintain.

This should not really come as a surprise. Top-down design -- as we discussed it in Chapter 3 -- does not really tell us *how* to break a large system into smaller pieces. And it does not tell us what kind of intermodule interfaces are preferable. In general, it lacks the formal guidelines that enable us to design systems in such a way that one module can be debugged, maintained, or modified without having to know anything about other modules -- and certainly without having to modify the code in any other modules.

This is not to suggest that top-down design is *bad;* indeed, some people have designed some very good systems using nothing more than the informal guidelines of top-down design. The reason for their success is (a) top-down design is certainly preferable to *no* design, which is the common situation in many organizations today, and (b) some programmers instinctively do *good* top-down design, without even knowing what they are doing.

All of this should provide an introduction to structured design. *Structured design* can be thought of as a collection of five related concepts, two of which are discussed in other chapters of this book:

- o *Documentation techniques.* Structured design includes some graphic tools which emphasize the structural, or hierarchical, aspects of a system rather than the procedural (loops and decisions) aspects. This area, which includes HIPO and structure charts, is discussed in Chapter 6.

- o *Theory.* Structured design also consists of some theory that helps us distinguish between "good" systems and "bad" systems -- at the module level.

- o *Heuristics.* Structured design includes a collection of rules of thumb which are useful when evaluating the "goodness" of a particular design -- but which should not be followed religiously.

- o *Design strategies.* Structured design also consists of various design "strategies" which allow us to systematically derive "good" solutions to common types of data processing problems. Top-down design could be thought of as one such strategy, though it is usually considered less useful than some of the other ones that are available.

- o *Implementation strategies.* Finally, structured design is considered by many to include the question of "implementation strategies": Given that we have a good design, in what order should we code and implement the modules? It is at this point that we discuss top-down implementation, bottom-up implementation, and some of the other issues that were raised in Chapter 3.

We do not have the opportunity in this book to discuss all of the technical theory, heuristics, and design strategies in detail; the references at the end of the chapter should be consulted for more information. However, we can give a brief example that will illustrate the philosophy behind structured design -- and we can then give a brief definition of some of the technical concepts.

To illustrate the philosophy of structured design, put yourself in the position of a management consultant. Suppose that you were asked to render an opinion on a company whose organization chart is shown in Figure 4.1. What would your reaction be? Most likely, you would comment that Vice-President A, and Manager X, and Manager Y all have trivial jobs -- since their responsibility seems to consist solely of managing one subordinate. Being a cynic, you would probably suggest that all of the work in that department is being done by Z, and that all of the managers should be fired!

Similarly, suppose you were asked to evaluate a company whose organization chart is shown in Figure 4.2. What would your reaction be? Chances are that you would predict trouble: The boss is a good candidate for an ulcer or a heart attack; at the very least, one would expect the boss to make a number of mistakes -- simply because he has too many people to manage.

Finally, suppose you were shown the organization chart in Figure 4.3. This looks much more reasonable! Each manager has a reasonable number of immediate subordinates -- a reasonable span of control -- and the entire organization seems properly "balanced." While there may be other problems in this company, at least the "architecture" indicated by the organization chart is reasonable.

Note that this does *not* mean that all good companies must have exactly three Vice-Presidents, as the company in Figure 4.3 happens to have. Nor are we suggesting that perfect symmetry is required: Just because Vice-President A has two immediate subordinates, we do not suggest that Vice-President B must also have two immediate subordinates. All we are saying is that Figure 4.1 and Figure 4.2 showed evidence of some structural problems -- and that Figure 4.3 does *not* show such evidence of trouble.

Why did we go into this example in such detail? Because *program* structures and *system* structures can be discussed in a similar way. Figures 4.1, 4.2, and 4.3 might well be structural representations of three different programs -- or three different *systems*, since the distinction between programs and systems is largely artificial at this level of abstraction.

Thus, we should be in a position to make some *structural* criticism of the program/system shown in Figure 4.1. It consists of a top-level "executive" module, which accomplishes the overall application by calling upon three "vice-president" modules. Our concern, of course, is with module A: From Figure 4.1, we get the strong suspicion that it consists of a single instruction -- a subroutine call to module X. Similarly, we suspect that module X contains only one instruction: a call to subroutine Y. And we suspect that module Y is a one-instruction module that does nothing but call module Z. Module Z, we suspect, is where all the work is done.

Figure 4.1: Representational company organization chart.

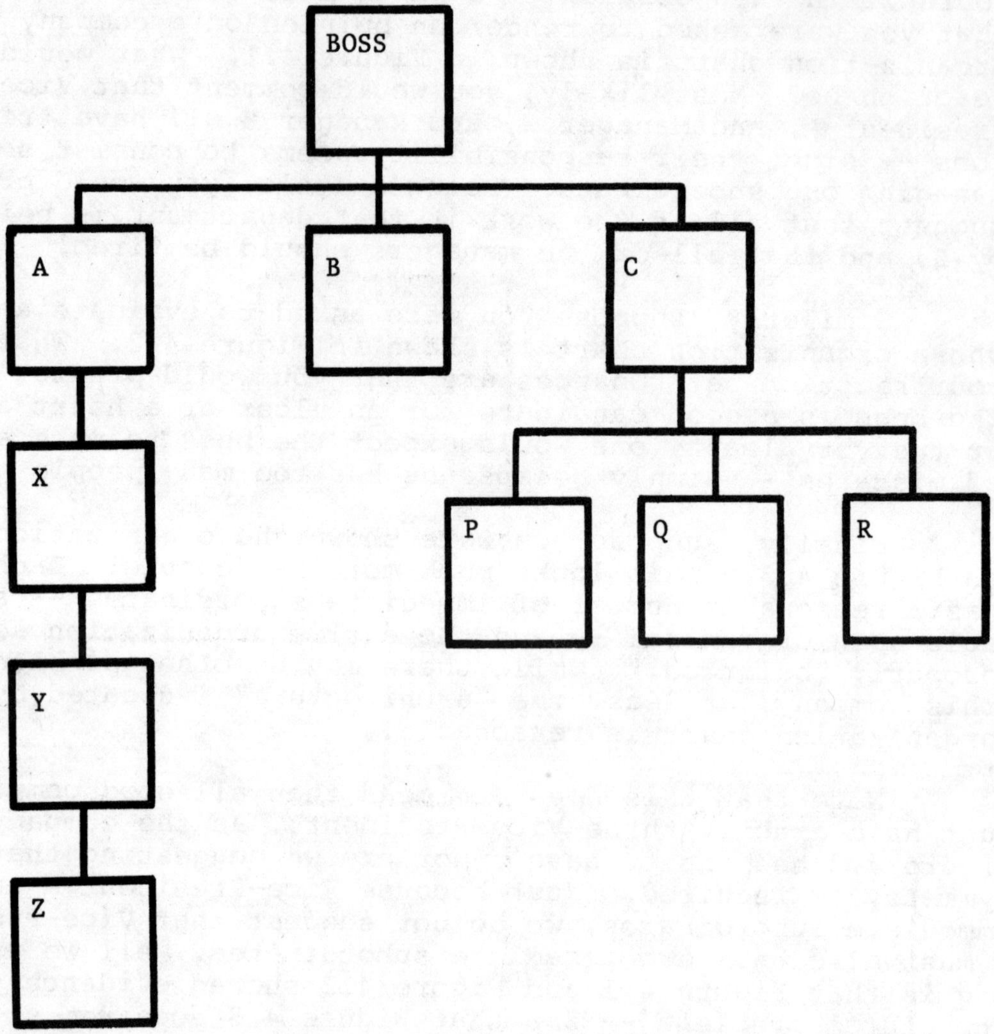

Figure 4.2: Representational organization chart of company 2.

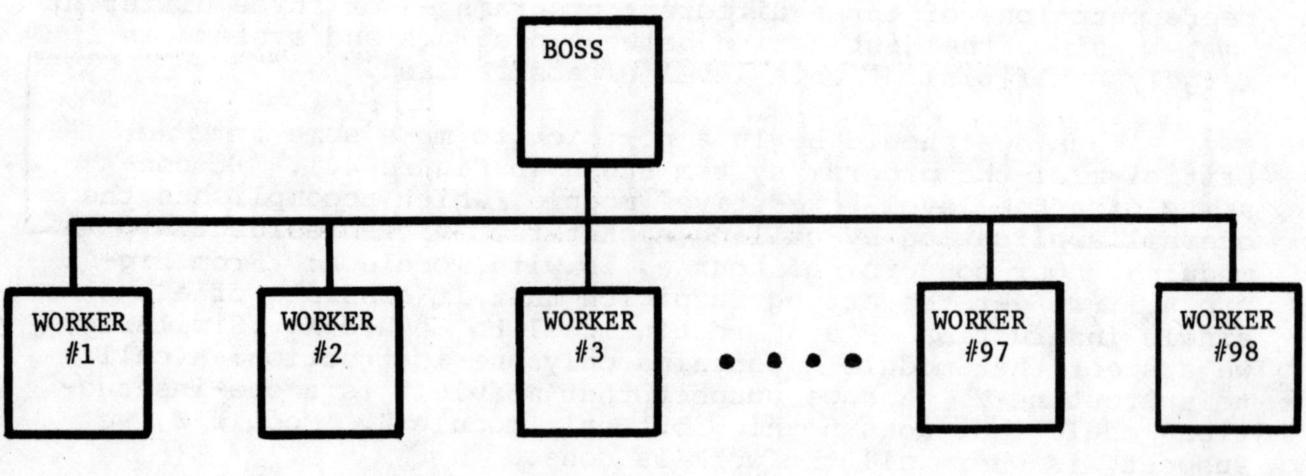

Figure 4.3: Representational company organization chart.

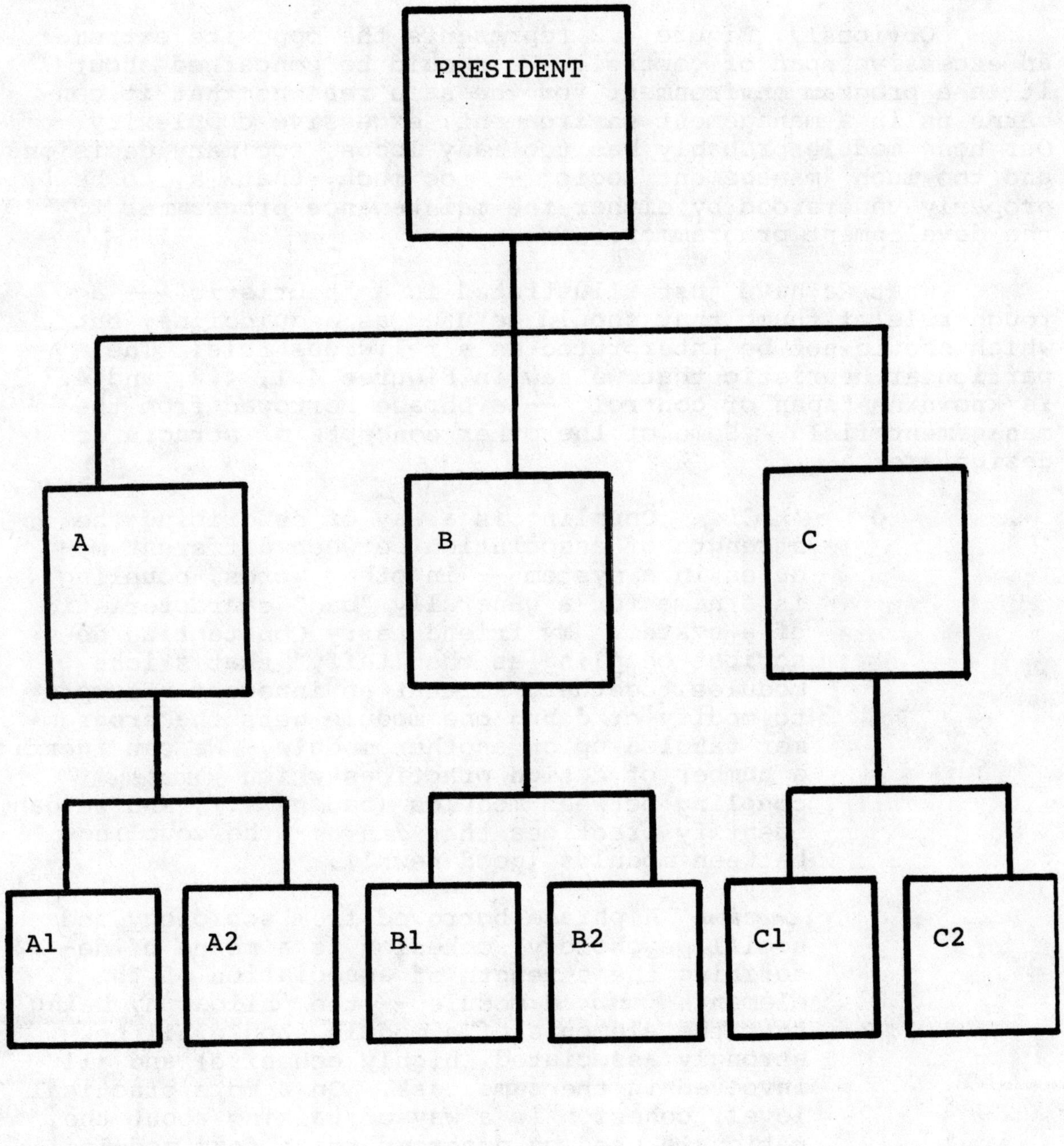

All of this must be kept in a certain perspective. We *suspect* that modules A, X, and Y are trivial -- but we don't really know unless we look at the code. And we recognize that there is nothing disastrously wrong with having a series of one-instruction subroutines which do nothing but call a lower-level module. It's just that such a structure is ... well, what should we call it? Trivial? Bureaucratic? Inefficient? All of these suggest that there is probably a better alternative to Figure 4.1.

Obviously, Figure 4.2 represents the opposite extreme: an excessive span of control. We should be concerned about it in a program environment for the same reasons that it concerns us in a management environment: excessive complexity. Our boss module probably has too many loops, too many decisions, and too much "management logic" -- too much, that is, to be properly understood by either the maintenance programmer *or* the development programmer.

What we have just illustrated is a "heuristic" -- a rough rule of thumb that should be used as a guideline, but which should not be interpreted as a religious rule. The particular heuristic that we saw in Figures 4.1, 4.2, and 4.3 is known as "span of control" -- a phrase borrowed from the management field. Some of the other concepts of structured design are:

- *Coupling.* Coupling is a way of describing the strength of association between different modules in a system -- in other words, coupling is a name for a generally "bad" characteristic of a system. My friend Larry Constantine describes coupling as the "taffy" that sticks modules together, so that an innocent attempt to modify or debug one module gets the programmer tangled up on another module. We can identify a number of design practices which *increase* coupling between modules (bad news!), and we can identify practices that *decrease* the coupling between modules (good news!).

- *Cohesion.* A phrase borrowed from sociology and social psychology, cohesion is a means of describing the strength of association of the elements *inside* a module -- the philosophy being that the elements of a module should all be strongly associated (highly cohesive) and all involved in the same task. On a more practical level, cohesion is a way of talking about the rationale used by programmers to form modules. We find that we can identify several useful levels of cohesion, some of which are "good" and some of which are "bad." The ultimate objective of cohesion is to show programmers how to form "good" modules, all of whose instructions are essential to the performance of one, *and only one,* task.

- *Pathological connections.* A pathological connection is one of the strongest forms of coupling between modules. Technically, a pathological connection is a reference from one module to the "insides" of another module. We find that pathological connections can be avoided if (a) a subroutine executes only as a result of a formal call from a superordinate, (b) the subroutine operates only on data given to it by its superordinate, (c) the subroutine is given only that data essential to the performance of its task, and (d) the subroutine delivers all of its outputs -- or results -- back to its superordinate.

- *Transform-centered design.* Transform-centered design is one of several design strategies that help the designer/programmer systematically derive good solutions to common types of applications. Transform-centered design requires the designer to study the *flow* of data through the system, and uses that as the basis for determining which modules will be required and how the modules will be organized hierarchically. Other design strategies, such as the one proposed by Michael Jackson,* require the designer to study the *structure* of the input data and output data, as a means of determining the program structure.

- *Packaging.* Packaging is a useful term for describing the decisions that the designer must ultimately make to "shoe-horn" his "logical" modules into the physical environment provided by the computer hardware, the vendor's operating system, and the programming language. One of the main philosophies of structured design is that packaging should be delayed as long as possible -- partly because it obscures the basic nature of the design problem, and partly because it leads to gross inefficiencies if accomplished too early.

---

*See Jackson's book, listed in the references for Chapter 4.

4.2 Management Problems with Structured Design

The last few pages have provided only the briefest overview of structured design, and I strongly suggest that you provide your designer/programmers with much more than such a brief overview before you expect them to put the ideas into practice.

Even with a reasonable amount of training and study, designer/programmers probably will experience some problems with their first few attempts to use structured design. The most common problems seem to be:

1. The designer's inability to grasp abstract design philosophies and concepts

2. Conflicts between the old "classical" design philosophies and the new "structured" philosophies

3. Difficulty enforcing formal design disciplines on small or medium-sized projects

4. Complaints of inefficiency

5. Difficulty defining the proper role of analyst, designer, and programmer.

Each of these problem areas is discussed separately below.

4.2.1 Designers' problems grasping abstract design philosophies

The overview of structured design earlier in this chapter may have made it seem like a simple concept. Don't be fooled: Many of your programmers and designers will find it quite difficult. Perhaps this is as it should be: Design *is* hard, and it will *never* be a trivial job to design a large system.

Nevertheless, the structured design techniques *do* work, and they *can* be used by people with a reasonable degree of intelligence. This may pose a management problem, however: You may find that the use of structured design requires more talented people than the ones currently doing your design.

This comment is not meant to be snide or cynical -- I have no interest in insulting you or your staff, even in a textbook! My comment is based on observing several thousands of programmers, designers, and analysts to whom I have tried to teach top-down design, structured design, and structured programming over the past few years. I find that most of them grasp top-down design and structured programming without too much trouble -- but, in many cases, structured design goes right over their heads.

Part of the problem may be one of terminology. Structured design introduces the terms "cohesion," "coupling," "pathological connections," "heuristics," and "transform-centered design," as we saw earlier in this chapter. A deeper discussion of the subject would add a number of additional buzz-words: afferent modules, efferent modules, temporally cohesive modules, procedurally cohesive modules, and so forth. Perhaps we should not be surprised to see some programmers throw up their hands in despair and walk away from structured design!

This poses a dilemma: On the one hand, we don't want to introduce new buzz-words in a field already overloaded with them. On the other hand, we *do* need words to describe certain technical aspects of computer systems design that have not been described before -- and we do *not* want to use words that have vendor-dependent meanings (e.g., the word "task" means something different depending on which programming language you use, which operating system you use, and which hardware you use). In fact, most of the buzz-words in structured design have been borrowed from other fields (e.g., "span of control," "cohesion," and "afferent" were borrowed from the fields of management science, sociology, and biology, respectively).

Even with all this apology for the buzz-words, we are left with a problem. Perhaps the best illustration of this is the *substantial* number of programmers who have asked me, in the middle of a training course on structured design, "By the way, what's a heuristic? I've never heard of the word." Understanding the concepts of structured design *does* require a certain grasp of the English language, and this seems a rather dangerous assumption to make with many programmers.

There is more to it than that. We can provide all programmers with a dictionary definition of the word "heuristic," or we can simply eliminate the word "heuristic," and substitute "rule of thumb," or "guideline." Even so, we *still* have problems.

Why? Primarily because most of the programmers and designers I have met feel an incredible urge to define everything in terms of religious principles. Even a simple guideline like "span of control" -- which we discussed earlier in this chapter -- becomes a religious principle.

Indeed, I have seen some programming groups *insist* that all programs have the kind of "symmetric" structure shown in Figure 4.3. Thus, the programmers are told that every system *must* contain one top-level module; that it *must* contain exactly three second-level modules, whose names will be "input," "process," and "output"; that if the "input" second-level module has two immediate subordinates beneath it, then the "process" and "output" modules also must have two immediate subordinates. And so on...

In the same fashion, we find programmers who interpret the concepts of coupling, cohesion, pathological connections, and transform-centered design in terms of ultimate "good" and ultimate "evil." Modules with low cohesion *must* be evil, and modules with high cohesion *must* be good; pathological connections *must* be bad; and so forth.

There is very little advice that I can give here, other than the obvious: Hire intelligent people. Make them read some of the available literature on the subject. Send them to any available conferences, symposia, workshops, or training sessions to learn the techniques. Make them talk out loud with their colleagues. And make them recognize that structured design is a form of common sense, not a new religion.

4.2.2 Conflicts between old design philosophies and new "structured" philosophies

Even if your programmers know what they're doing, there is likely to be a problem introducing the new structured design techniques. The problem is that your organization probably has design standards that seriously conflict with the structured design philosophies.

On the simplest level, I have seen organizations -- even today, in the late 1970's -- that have outlawed subroutine calls. PERFORM statements, CALL statements, procedure calls, BALR instructions in IBM System/370 assembly language -- all outlawed. That makes it a little difficult to institute structured design!

More commonly, I have seen problems in the area of cohesion, packaging, and pathological connections. The organizational standards may dictate, for example, that every program have a "general-purpose-edit-module" and a "general-purpose-error-routine." While the standards are obviously well-intentioned, structured design would argue against such modules, on the grounds that they represent classic examples of "logical cohesion."* Similarly, the organizational standards may require the programmer to develop a "master file control"

---

*Logical cohesion describes a module that contains many similar functions -- which is quite a different thing from a module that carries out one single function. What concerns us is that the code for those many similar functions may become intertwined in such a way that a subsequent attempt to modify one of the functions will inadvertently damage or destroy one of the other functions in the same module. For a deeper discussion, see the references at the end of the chapter.

module for his program -- i.e., a module that, depending on the nature of a flag passed to it, will either open the master file, close the master file, read the master file, or carry out any of a number of other similar functions on the master file. Structured design would reject that standard, too, on the grounds that it represents a classic example of "communicational cohesion."

Many of our organizational standards were developed five or ten years ago, when things were very different than they are today. In particular, many such standards were created for the sake of machine efficiency -- which, as we will discuss further in Section 4.2.4, are largely irrelevant today.

So, what should you do as a manager? Be prepared for some conflicts. And be prepared to scrap some of your obsolete standards!

4.2.3 Difficulty enforcing the discipline of structured design on small projects

After they have tried it once or twice, your programmers will be happy to tell you that a proper application of cohesion, coupling, transform-centered design, and all the rest of structured design *takes a lot of time*.

To appreciate this, imagine how your programmers would react if you asked them to write a simple sequential file update program in COBOL. Normally, the program would require two- or three-hundred COBOL statements -- but now suppose that you have decided to enforce the following "religious rules" of structured design:

1. The update program must be broken into modules, no one of which can be longer than one page of a listing.

2. All modules must be invoked with a CALL statement. PERFORM statements are not allowed.

3. No module is allowed to "remember" anything from one execution to the next. This means no "first-time" switches, and no internal state maintenance.

4. No "manager" module is allowed to do any work. That is, any module that is not at the bottom of the hierarchy must consist only of CALL statements imbedded within loops and decisions.

Actually, these rules are quite reasonable for medium-sized and large-sized projects -- but you can imagine how your programmers would squawk if you imposed such rules on a 200-statement COBOL application.

Obviously, only you (or the standards department!) can decide how formal you want to be. If your programmers work individually on small programs that require only a day or two of work -- then some of the philosophies behind structured design may be useful, but I wouldn't bother with the formality. On medium-sized projects -- those requiring two or three programmers for a few months -- some of the formality of structured design is appropriate, but one does not have to be a fanatic about it. On *big* projects, one *should* be a fanatic -- we need all the help we can get on big systems!

Be careful of one thing: Many programming projects *appear* to be one-person projects, when in fact they are really small pieces of a large, integrated system. Many organizations have worked for years on the theory that a big system can be broken into small pieces, each of which can be worked on by individual programmers as if they were independent projects. That is quite true, of course -- but we must not forget that the principles of structured design are essential if we are to do a good job of breaking the system into small independent pieces.

Also, keep in mind that the maintenance costs of a lot of small programs will eventually add up. Even if it does take considerably longer to develop a small program with the formality of structured design, it may be worth the effort -- just to make the program more maintainable.

4.2.4 Complaints of inefficiency

Many programmers (and managers!!) are still thinking in second-generation terms, when every microsecond was important and every byte of memory was to be cherished as a precious national resource.

To such people, various aspects of structured design may be anathema. The extensive use of subroutines suggests a certain degree of inefficiency; the emphasis on highly cohesive modules suggests even more inefficiency; and the suggestion that data be passed through a parameter list (instead of being placed in a globally accessible area) usually raises howls of anguish from programmers.

Obviously, nobody wants a grossly inefficient system. Obviously, efficiency is important in some cases -- as in real-time systems, or systems with high volumes of processing. Nevertheless, we can usually argue that most of the hue and cry about efficiency is irrelevant in today's computer systems.

As a manager, you should keep the following points in mind:

1. In most cases, you don't know whether your computer systems are efficient or inefficient -- and neither does the computer operations manager. More significant: Nobody really *cares* if most programs are inefficient. If your programmer writes a program that consumes one minute of machine time, does anybody know whether it could have been written in such a way that it would consume only 30 seconds of CPU time? Does anybody care?

2. Efficiency seems to be influenced more by the quality of the programmer than by any specific techniques of structured design. Recall the Sackman experiment that we discussed in Chapter 2 -- picking the right programmer can improve the efficiency of your systems by a factor of ten.

3. Most informal surveys have suggested that diligent use of structured design adds an overhead of about 10% to the CPU time and memory requirements of a program. The reason we refer to "informal surveys" is that very few people have attempted the kind of study that Sackman attempted. Indeed, to *really* determine the cost of structured design, we would have to take a pair of identical twins and have them work on the same problem -- one using techniques of structured design and one using the classical approach. I am not aware of any such experiment, though I would be happy to organize one if any identical twins would like to volunteer!

4. A number of studies have confirmed that the "90-10" rule applies to programs, too. That is, 10% of the code in a typical system will consume 90% of the CPU time; Knuth showed in a study in the April 1971 issue of *Software -- Practice & Experience* that 5% of the code consumed 50% of the CPU time. In other words, only a small amount of the code is significant; so the strategy should be to get the system working, then find out which parts are inefficient (if anyone cares), and then optimize it.

5. In general, it is easier to make a correct system efficient than it is to make an efficient system correct. Get the system working *first*. *Then* worry about efficiency.

6.6. Programmers, according to a study conducted by my colleague P.J. Plauger, are notoriously poor at anticipating in advance *which* 5% of their code will be inefficient. They frequently blame their efficiency problems on the part of the system they found most difficult to design and code -- but the problem usually turns out to be some innocent-looking module that is chewing up 75% of the CPU time.

4.2.5 Difficulty defining the proper role of analyst, designer, and programmer

One of the unfortunate aspects of structured design is that it has identified an organizational problem in many data processing departments. To put it simply, *systems analysts* spend most of their time talking to the user, and occasionally do a little design; *programmers* spend most of their time writing COBOL statements, and occasionally do a little design. But nobody does any *serious* design!

As a result, nobody is really sure whether structured design is something that the systems analyst should learn, or something that the programmer should learn. Our answer is: *Both* groups should learn structured design, since it is applicable to systems analysis (more on this in Chapter 14), systems design, and program design.

In addition, many organizations would be well advised to create a new person in the EDP department; for lack of a better title, I'll call this new person the "systems architect." The reason for suggesting a new person is that (a) there is a vacuum in the design area of most companies today, and (b) most of the analysts and programmers I meet are incompetent to fill the role without some serious changes to the way they do their jobs.

This is particularly apparent in the case of systems analysts. Many systems analysts have arrived in their current position after spending years in the "user" area of the organization. Thus, while they are quite competent to describe the user's business and the user's problem (a crucially valuable skill, to be sure!!), they don't know a computer from a football -- and it shows in their designs!

Other systems analysts spent the formative years of their career working on second-generation machines like the IBM 1401 -- and having risen to their current exalted position of systems analyst, they *still* design systems as if they were working on an IBM 1401. It is this group, in particular, that is guilty of premature packaging -- that is, chopping a system into distinct programs at the very beginning of the project, and dictating that all information will be passed from program to program via magnetic tape. And all of this on a 4-megabyte 370/168 that is capable of holding *all* of the code in memory at once, and capable of passing all of the data from module to module through core memory....

Meanwhile, the programmers in many organizations have never had the opportunity (or perhaps never shown the talent) to carry out any real *design*. They expect to be given a design, from which they can happily figure out which assortment of COBOL statements will most befuddle the maintenance programmer.

So, maybe we *do* need a new breed of person in our organization. Maybe we should distinguish between "business systems design" (talking to the user to find out what he wants), "computer system design" (determining the structure of modules that will solve a well-specified problem), and "programming" (carrying out the detailed procedural design of each module).

Chapter 4: References

1. Dijkstra, Edsger, *A Discipline of Programming*, Prentice-Hall, 1976.

2. Jackson, Michael, *Principles of Program Design*, Academic Press, 1975.

3. Myers, Glenford J., *Reliable Software Through Composite Design*, Petrocelli/Charter, 1975.

4. Stevens, W.G.; G.J. Myers, and L.L. Constantine, "Structured Design," *IBM Systems Journal*, May 1974.

5. Wirth, Niklaus, *Algorithms + Data Structures = Programs*, Prentice-Hall, 1976.

6. Yourdon, Edward, and Larry Constantine, *Structured Design*, YOURDON inc., 1975.

Chapter 5 HOW TO MANAGE STRUCTURED PROGRAMMING

Having discussed top-down design and structured design, we now turn to a "lower-level" topic: programming. Specifically, this chapter is devoted to a discussion of *structured programming* -- the technique often regarded as the first of the PPT techniques.

In keeping with the theme of previous chapters, we will begin with a brief technical overview of structured programming. Most of our discussion, though, will be concerned with the problems you will have implementing structured programming in your organization.

5.1 An Overview of Structured Programming

The term "structured programming" was coined by Professor Edsger Dijkstra in the mid-1960's, and first came to the attention of a significant number of people at a NATO Software Engineering conference in 1968. From that point on, it has been widely studied and discussed in academic circles; indeed, most of the good computer science schools (universities, that is) teach structured programming as the students' first introduction to programming.

Meanwhile, IBM -- after being exposed to structured programming at that 1968 NATO conference -- adopted the technique on an experimental basis on a project that has come to be known as "the New York Times system" (see the reference by F.T. Baker at the end of this chapter). Finding it a tremendously successful technique, IBM spread it through its own organization -- and from there to their many customers. Indeed, IBM's influence is probably one of the major reasons why you are reading this book!

So, what *is* structured programming? From a technical point of view, one could describe it as the theoretical basis for all procedural logic -- that is, for the kind of logic that we have traditionally described with a flowchart. In the mid-1960's, two Italian computer scientists, Böhm and Jacopini, proved mathematically that any procedural logic (that is, any flowchart) could be derived from combinations of three basic kinds of flowcharts shown in Figure 5.1.

These three flowcharts really form the "core" of structured programming. They are popularly referred to as "sequence," "IFTHENELSE," and "DOWHILE." The discovery that these three are sufficient for any arbitrarily complex logic structure is profoundly important -- just as important as the hardware engineer's discovery that any form of hardware logic can be constructed from combinations of AND gates, OR gates, and NOT gates.

Not only are the three flowchart elements in Figure 5.1 simple but they also have the desirable property of being "black-box" in nature. That is, they are all characterized by having a single entry point, and a single exit point. This, too, is profoundly important: It means that we can take a program whose flowchart has been constructed from the three basic forms and examine any part of it as a "stand-alone" black-box. This is in sharp contrast to the flowcharts for conventional programs, which wander willy-nilly from page to page -- to the point where neither the development programmer nor the maintenance programmer has the faintest idea what the logic is doing.

Note that our discussion thus far has been in terms of *flowcharts* -- a documentation tool which, as we will discuss in Chapter 6, has largely been abandoned in most organizations. Part of the reason for leading into structured programming in this way is that flowcharts are clean and simple -- they're language-independent and vendor-independent! The other reason is that structured programming *was* developed in this way: The Böhm and Jacopini paper that provided the theoretical basis for structured programming used flowcharts, rather than a specific programming language.

However, most of our programmers *do* use specific programming languages -- COBOL, FORTRAN, PL/I, assembly language, and a vast number of lesser dialects (ALGOL, APL, RPG, BASIC, SNOBOL, LISP, and on and on...). So, our next question is: What does structured programming mean in terms of *real* programming languages?

Quite simply, it means that we should write instructions that are direct implementations of the flowcharts shown in Figure 5.1. Obviously, all programming languages have a variety of simple instructions, and the capability to arrange them in a linear sequence -- so that is no problem.

All programming languages also have some facility for making binary decisions -- although not all make it easy to program the kind of decision structure shown in Figure 5.1, in which control returns to a common point. What we need is a language that implements the verb IF-THEN-ELSE. And since we want the ability to build combinations of these structures, we want a programming language that allows us to code *nested* IF-THEN-ELSE structures.

Finally, we want our programming language to give us the facility for forming loops -- especially simple loops of the form shown in Figure 5.1. In languages like ALGOL and PL/I, such a loop is implemented directly with the verb DO-WHILE. In less formal languages like COBOL, we can use the verbs PERFORM-UNTIL and PERFORM-VARYING. In primitive languages like FORTRAN, we are given only the special "iterative" loop -- the well-known FORTRAN DO loop.

Figure 5.1

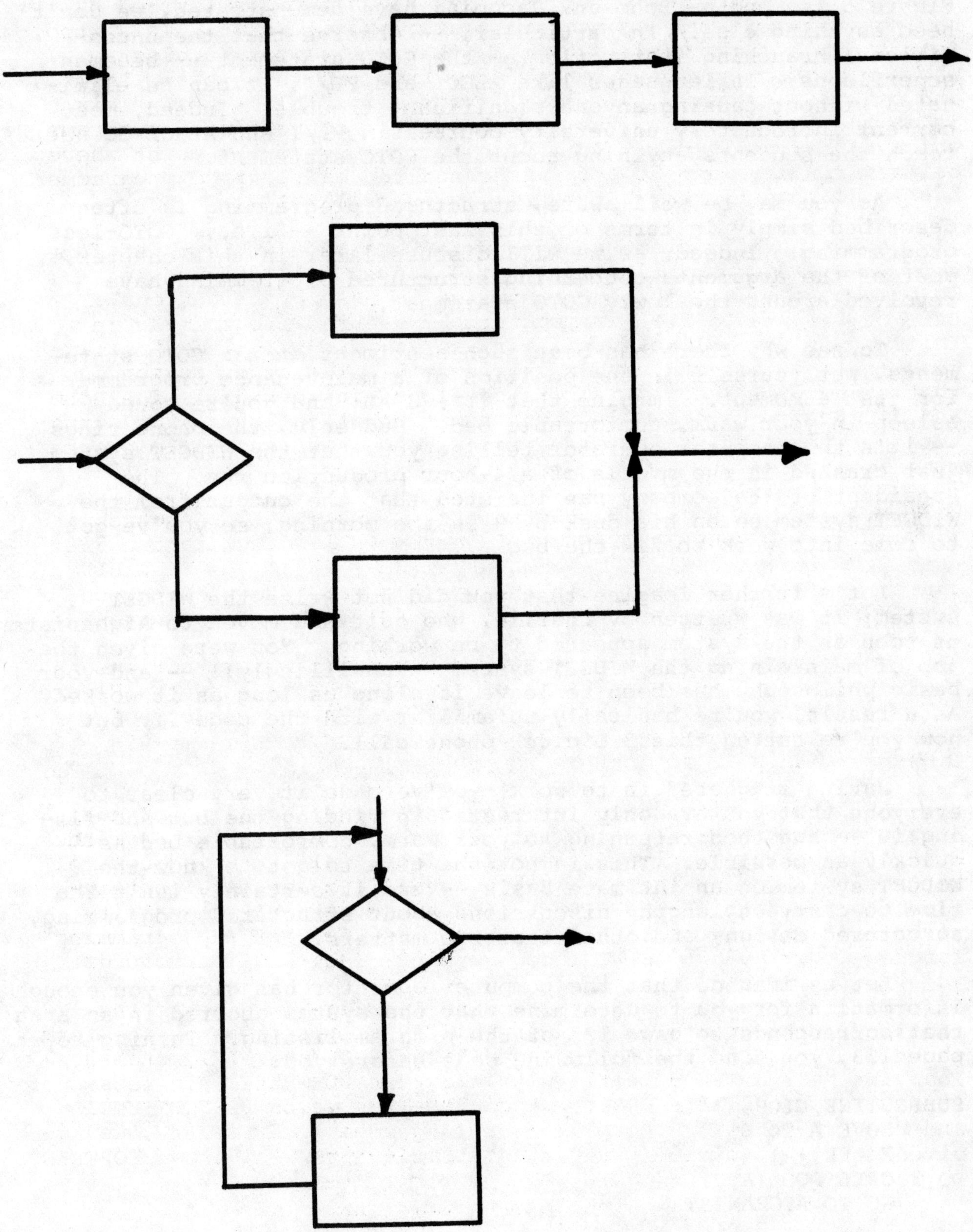

In the more powerful programming languages, we find that we have all of the verbs with which to implement the flowcharts of Figure 5.1. And as Bohm and Jacopini have demonstrated, we don't need anything else! In particular, we observe that the unconditional branching instruction -- the GOTO statement -- becomes superfluous. In languages like ALGOL and PL/I, it can be eliminated without causing anyone significant trouble. Indeed, most current introductory university courses in PL/I and ALGOL do not teach the students anything about the GOTO statement.

As you may be well aware, structured programming is often described simply in terms of this last point -- i.e., "GOTO-less" programming. Indeed, as we will discuss later in this chapter, most of the arguments concerning structured programming have revolved around the lowly GOTO statement.

To see why there has been such sentiment *against* GOTO statements, put yourself in the position of a maintenance programmer for just a moment. Imagine that it's 3 AM, and you're sound asleep in your warm, comfortable bed. Suddenly, the phone rings -- it's the computer operator telling you that the WIDGET system just crashed in the middle of a 4-hour production run. The President of the company has insisted that the output from the WIDGET system be on his desk by 9 in the morning, so you've got to come into work to fix the bug....

Let's further imagine that you did not write the WIDGET system; it was written by Charlie, who quit and moved to Afghanistan as soon as the system appeared to be working. You were given the job of maintaining the WIDGET system -- unwillingly!! -- and your basic philosophy has been to leave it alone as long as it worked. As a result, you're basically unfamiliar with the code ... but now you've gotten this 3 o'clock phone call.

Having staggered in to work, you've made it very clear to everyone that you are only interested in finding the bug and fixing it -- and then returning to your warm, comfortable bed as quickly as possible. This is not the time to get to know the WIDGET system on an intimate basis -- and it certainly isn't the time to carry on lengthy discussions about structured programming, structured design, and other esoteric matters.

Let us imagine that the computer operator has given you enough information for you to determine that the system aborted in an area that corresponds to page 123 of the program listing. Turning to page 123, you find the following code before you:

```
SUBROUTINE GLOP
     MOVE A TO B
     X = X + 1
     CALL FOO (A,B)
     GO TO AFGHANISTAN
     .
     .
     .
```

Of course, your first question is: What does GLOP do? What is its purpose? The ideal situation would be to find that page 123 of the program listing is the beginning of some recognizable *function* -- e.g., computing an employee's gross salary, or converting a BCD character string to an ASCII character string -- which would have been *finished* by the time we reached the bottom of page 123. But such is probably not the case with subroutine GLOP....

Undaunted, you begin reading the code (note that, in order to avoid offending anyone, I've included a mixture of COBOL, FORTRAN, and PL/I). The very first statement, as you can see, causes the contents of a variable named "A" to be moved to a variable named "B". That seems simple enough, and you would be inclined to shrug your shoulders and move on to the next instruction.

However, there are some important things to understand about that MOVE statement. First of all, you have unconsciously *assumed* that the MOVE statement will do what it's supposed to do. If you were a very paranoid maintenance programmer, you might possibly double-check to ensure that the compiler generated the proper object code for that MOVE statement; and if you were *very* paranoid, you might even check the hardware to ensure that it was executing the assembly language instructions properly.

But the chances are, you aren't that paranoid. And besides, it's 3 o'clock in the morning, and all you want to do is find the bug and go home. From the evidence that the computer operator gave you, you have reason to suspect that the bug is somewhere in the logic on page 123 -- and there is no reason to descend to the lower levels of assembly language or machine language unless you have to.

So, once again, you are probably ready to read on past the MOVE statement. But wait! We have two more things to say about that innocent MOVE. First of all, note that the MOVE statement has the following interesting property: When it finishes MOVEing, the computer goes on to the next instruction. Trivial as that point may seem, *that* is what we depend on in order to be able to ignore the details of the assembly language code that follow the MOVE statement.

Also, note that there is *some* investigation that you could do -- and probably *should* do -- concerning the MOVE statement. It is reasonable to ask, for example, "*Why* are we moving A to B? Why are we doing it now? What is the purpose, the rationale, behind that instruction? Why did Charlie do it?"

Assuming that you could answer these questions, *then* you might examine the next statement. Evidently, it increments a variable X by one. Aside from that, it has the same desirable properties as the MOVE statement: Its details can be ignored for the present time; the instruction can be assumed to function correctly for the moment; and it can be assumed that, having incremented X by one, the computer will move on to the next instruction.

The next instruction is a bit more interesting. As you can see, it reads

```
CALL FOO (A,B)
```

Unfortunately, it is not clear what is happening -- other than the obvious fact that a subroutine named FOO is being invoked, and two parameters, A and B, are being passed to it.

At this point, you might be strongly tempted to search through the program listing to find subroutine FOO -- to find out what FOO is doing. Wrong!! To become involved in the details of subroutine FOO is to destroy much of what we have accomplished with the philosophy of top-down design, structured design, and structured programming.

The point is that FOO probably carries out some kind of *function* -- although the nature of that function is certainly not clear from the name FOO. Let us assume, though, that Charlie left a minimal amount of documentation behind, and that you are able to quickly discover (without finding FOO in the program listing) that the purpose of FOO is to compute the square root of its first argument, and return the answer in the second argument.

That's all we need to know! At this point, we should *assume* that FOO computes square roots correctly -- *just as we assumed that the MOVE statement works correctly*. If you are ultimately unable to find the bug on page 123, *then* you may be tempted to explore the logic of FOO -- but in the meantime, it's 3 in the morning and common sense dictates that you restrict your attention *solely* to the logic on page 123.

Note that, as with the MOVE statement, there are some intelligent questions that you should ask concerning FOO. Namely: "Why compute a square root at this point? Does it make sense to compute the square root of A? Do I really want to store the answer in B?" Indeed, *these* questions might uncover the bug on page 123 -- and it is *this* kind of top-down debugging that we wish to emphasize.

Having laid the groundwork for all of this, *now* you can see why the GOTO statement is such a disaster. Immediately after the CALL FOO statement (which, by the way, you *assumed* would return!), you see a statement that says

```
GO TO AFGHANISTAN
```

Ho! ho! ho! Probably the last statement Charlie wrote before he departed ... but at 3 in the morning, the humor wears a little thin. In particular, you find yourself asking the following pertinent questions:

1. Where is AFGHANISTAN in the 800-page program listing?

2. Why are we going to AFGHANISTAN?

3. What are we going to do when we get to AFGHANISTAN?

4. Will we ever get back to the code on page 123?

Unfortunately, these are questions that *cannot* be avoided. It may well be that the instructions at AFGHANISTAN are only minor details -- but there is no way that you can know that, and no way that you can avoid finding out, as you were able to do with the FOO subroutine.

Thus, you are forced to track down the location of AFGHANISTAN in the program listing -- a possibly tedious effort in itself. Chances are, AFGHANISTAN is far away (no pun intended!) from the code at page 123; suppose, for example, it turns out that AFGHANISTAN is on page 786. At that point, you would do three things:

1. Stick one finger in the listing at page 123, in the faint hope that you might eventually get back there.

2. Carefully remember what the "state of the world" is at this point -- i.e., remember what variables A, B, and X contain.

3. Turn to page 786.

Imagine the following sort of code on page 786:

```
AFGHANISTAN.
        X = X+1
        MOVE B TO C
        GO TO MOZAMBIQUE
```

Once again, you start reading through the code. The first statement looks simple enough -- just another case of incrementing variable X. Let's see, now, what did X contain when you got to AFGHANISTAN? You tried to remember all of that before you turned to page 786, but at this hour, it's hard to remember very much... so you quickly turn back to page 123 (thank goodness you left your finger stuck in the listing!) to refresh your memory, and then back to page 786 again.

But wait! How do you know that the only way that the program gets to AFGHANISTAN is from the code on page 123? In other words, how do you *really* know what variable X contains when you begin executing instructions on page 786? Indeed, there may be a dozen -- or a hundred -- devious paths that lead to AFGHANISTAN....

At 3 AM, your temptation would be to ignore this unpleasant situation -- and therein lies the source of many a bug! If you decide to change that first instruction at AFGHANISTAN to something like

```
X = X+2
```

it may well work for the case you were following (i.e., from page 123), but you may have destroyed things for some other -- at this point completely unknown -- logic path that also ends up at AFGHANISTAN.

Indeed, your troubles are just beginning... for as you can see, AFGHANISTAN executes two relatively simple statements, and then uses a GOTO to disappear off to MOZAMBIQUE.

But where is MOZAMBIQUE? And why are we going there? What is the program going to do when it gets to MOZAMBIQUE? Not knowing the answer to these questions, you have no choice but to stick *another* finger in the program listing at page 786, and turn to yet another part of the listing....

I think you would agree that after three or four such GOTO statements, your temptation would be to give up. You've forgotten where you started, you've run out of fingers to stick in the listing to remind you where you've been, you don't know where you're going ... and you're getting very, very sleepy....

That, quite simply, is what structured programming is all about; or, to be more precise, that is the *antithesis* of structured programming. By eliminating GOTO statements -- especially the wild GOTOs that jump hundreds of pages in the program listing -- and by restricting ourselves to combinations of the three Böhm and Jacopini forms, we end up with code that can be read and understood, literally, from the top down. That is, we find that we begin reading code at the top of the page, continue reading it in a straight-line fashion, and by the time we reach the bottom of the page, we have finished doing something.

The result? First of all, it means that the development programmer can understand what he is doing (which our mythical friend Charlie, in the example above, probably didn't -- and *that* is probably one of the reasons he disappeared to Afghanistan!), which means that he can write more code with fewer bugs. That, in turn, means that the development programmer is more productive -- *and* that the code is more reliable.

Let's not underestimate the significance of that point. If the development programmer understands what he is doing, then the code will probably work. Which means that those phone calls at 3 in the morning will become a thing of the past. And, if the maintenance programmer *does* get one of those middle-of-the-night phone calls, it's more likely that (a) he can find the bug in a reasonable amount of time, and (b) he can fix the bug without introducing any new bugs.

So that's what structured programming is all about. For more details, you and/or your programmers should consult the references at the end of the chapter.

5.2 Management Problems with Structured Programming

By now you should be prepared for a section on "problem areas." We suggested in earlier chapters that programmers run into difficulties trying to implement top-down design, top-down testing, and structured design. Why should things be any easier with structured programming?

As a matter of fact, things are just the same -- that is, programmers *do* have trouble with structured programming, even though the concept is simple. There are nearly a dozen common problems for which you should be prepared:

1. Eternal arguments and battles over GOTO statements.
2. The myth that "GOTO-less" code is equivalent to "good" code.
3. Weaknesses in the syntax of such high-level programming languages as PL/I, COBOL, and FORTRAN.
4. Programmers' ignorance of their programming language.
5. Difficulties applying structured programming to assembly language on most computers.
6. Attitude problems with "old-timer" programmers.
7. Complaints of inefficiency with structured programming.
8. Conflicts with old programming standards.
9. Difficulty enforcing structured programming standards.
10. Difficulty using structured programming in a maintenance environment.
11. Problems with nested IF statements.

Let us now discuss each of these problem areas in turn.

5.2.1 Arguments over GOTO statements

The discussion in the previous section illustrated, I think, the major arguments *against* GOTO statements. It's not that I think -- or that Dijkstra, Mills, Wirth, Böhm, or Jacopini think -- that the GOTO statement is inherently evil. What concerns us is that the GOTO statement is *potentially* dangerous, and that it can *easily* lead to the kind of programming situation we described earlier.

Unfortunately, the issue of GOTO statements has become almost a religious one. To say, "I am writing structured programs" is considered equivalent to "I have cleverly managed to avoid writing any GOTO statements in my program."

By itself, that sort of religious mania might not be so bad. Unfortunately, there are times, in the "real world," when one desperately feels a need to write a GOTO statement. The major arguments *in favor* of GOTO statements seem to be:

1. There are times when the programming language makes it difficult -- if not impossible -- to describe a simple piece of logic without using a GOTO statement. We will have more to say about this in Section 5.2.3.

2. There are a few cases where a judiciously placed GOTO statement will greatly improve the efficiency of a program -- compared to the structured means of coding it.

3. One can occasionally argue that a GOTO statement is more readable than the equivalent structured code. A good case in point is the coding for a premature exit from the middle of a loop: Such a case *can* be coded in a structured fashion, but it requires extra switches and some clumsy-looking code.

4. Similarly, some programmers argue that GOTO statements are a more readable, more comprehensible alternative to nested IF statements. We will have more to say about this comment in Section 5.2.11.

5. There are times when the programmer simply can't figure out how to express some familiar logic in a structured form -- mainly because he has spent so many years flowcharting and/or coding that logic in an unstructured form.

The significant point is that none of this is worth a major battle. If the programmer seriously considers the alternative means of coding some logic, and if he sincerely believes that a GOTO statement makes the code more efficient, or more maintainable, or easier to understand -- then it is probably okay.

To put it another way: If proper attention has been paid to the concepts of top-down design and structured design discussed in Chapters 3 and 4, then the issue of GOTO statements is probably not so critical. If structured design concepts had been enforced, the AFGHANISTAN situation described earlier in this chapter would not have occurred: Charlie would have been required to design his system in terms of small, independent, highly cohesive, loosely coupled modules that could be coded on one page. Thus, there would be no GOTO statements jumping from page 123 to page 786 -- and if there were a few GOTO statements jumping around *within* page 123, the objections would not be all that significant.

So, my advice is: Don't let any arguments over GOTO statements go on for more than a few moments. *Do* make sure that your programmer knows how to express a particular piece of logic in a structured, GOTO-less fashion (if all else fails, there is something known as the Ashcroft-Manna technique, described in Chapter 4 of my *Techniques of Program Structure and Design*, referenced at the end of this chapter, guaranteed to give a programmer a structured means of expressing *any* logic) before he decides whether or not to actually use the GOTO statement.

5.2.2 The myth that structured code is "good" code

Just as there is a religious myth that GOTO statements are "bad," so there is a myth that structured, "GOTO-less," code *must* be "good" -- that is, by merely eliminating the GOTO statements from one's code, one is guaranteed to have readable, understandable, perfectly maintainable, error-free code.

Clearly, this is not the case. One can *always* write bad code if one tries hard enough. With or without GOTO statements, a programmer can construct obscure, hopelessly inefficient, perverse code. Indeed, you should watch out for this: If one of your programmers has decided that he doesn't like the idea of structured programming, he may deliberately write bad code in an attempt to demonstrate that structured programming is a bad idea.

In my experience, it is quite common for programmers to write structured code that is:

- *Inefficient*. Indeed, hopelessly inefficient. One of the classic cases of this was a programmer who wrote

```
DO I = 1 TO 3
    CASE I OF
        CASE 1
            A = 13
        CASE 2
            B = 75
        CASE 3
            C = 86
    END-CASE
END-DO
```

  when he could have written

```
A = 13
B = 75
C = 86
```

  (By the way, if that code isn't perfectly clear to you, get one of your programmers to explain it to you.) Such gross inefficiencies often occur as a result of a fatal fascination with all of the structured "verbs."

- *Incorrect*. Some programmers have a tendency to write structured code that has *more* bugs than their previous "unstructured" code. This is usually the result of weaknesses in the programming language (which we will discuss in Section 5.2.3) or the result of the programmer's ignorance of certain features of his programming language (see Section 5.2.4).

- *Obscure*. One could argue that the coding shown immediately above is a good example of obscure code. It is also common to see code that is obscure because the programmer tried to squeeze too many levels of nested loops and decisions onto one page of coding. Perhaps the worst offender, though, is the nested IF statement -- which we will discuss separately in Section 5.2.11.

To summarize: Structured programming is not a panacea. Your programmers are still capable of writing lousy code -- especially if they try!!

5.2.3 Weaknesses in high-level programming languages

Perhaps one of the most significant problems in structured programming is that the most common high-level programming languages interfere with the programmer's natural inclination to design and code structured logic. That criticism is only slightly valid with the PL/I programming language; it is reasonably valid with COBOL; and it is extremely appropriate in the case of FORTRAN.

The nature of this book makes it inappropriate to discuss language problems in detail. However, we can summarize some of the problems as follows:

- *PL/I.* PL/I *does* have a DO-WHILE statement, a nested IF-THEN-ELSE statement, formal block structures, and the concept of "local" variables that are only known within a limited domain. However, PL/I does *not* at the current time have a REPEAT-UNTIL structure, a CASE structure, or a BREAK facility to allow premature exits from loops. Thus, there are a few cases where PL/I coding is more clumsy than it should be -- but such situations are relatively rare.

- *COBOL.* In terms of structured programming, COBOL is a mediocre language at best. While it has a PERFORM-UNTIL statement to provide for GOTO-less loops, the body of the loop is required to be out-of-line, in contrast to the in-line DO-WHILE of PL/I. While it allows several statements to be included in one sentence, this kind of "block structure" is informal, and causes trouble when one tries to put blocks inside of other blocks. This causes severe problems when combined with the concept of nested IF statements -- problems that do not occur in other languages. In addition, COBOL lacks a CASE structure, lacks a REPEAT-UNTIL loop structure, and -- perhaps most important -- lacks the concept of local variables.

- *FORTRAN.* The most primitive of high-level programming languages, FORTRAN lacks any form of nested IF statement, and provides *no* IF-THEN-ELSE statement. It has a loop -- the DO loop -- but it is of the "iterative" variety, which covers only a small percentage of the looping applications required by programmers. It has no block structures, and its concept of local variables is primitive. A disaster of a language!

To write "perfect" structured code, I would have to advise you to program in languages like ALGOL or PASCAL. But that is roughly equivalent to telling you to carry on human conversations in Latin or Esperanto! In addition to the technical considerations of structured programming, you must deal with a number of other language considerations:

- Can you find a ready supply of programmers who are facile in language X? There is a large supply of COBOL programmers -- while far fewer programmers speak ALGOL.

- Can you train your existing programmers to code in language X? Teaching a new programming language to a veteran with several years of experience is much like trying to teach French to an adult American: one has to be prepared for a heavily accented mish-mash of both languages. It's not unusual to find veteran programmers who are still coding FORTRAN (or COBOL) logic in PL/I.

- Does your computer vendor support language X? Virtually every vendor has some reasonable implementation of COBOL, FORTRAN, and assembly language. At the time this book was written, only IBM could be depended upon for a decent version of PL/I -- though all the other vendors are talking about it. As for ALGOL -- most major computers have a version of ALGOL, but the vendor's software representatives (or "systems engineers") probably won't be able to give you much help.

So, chances are, you should stick with the language that you are currently using. Take solace from the fact that *all* of the major high-level languages have some weaknesses and clumsy features. Also, keep two other points in mind:

1. The official committees which define FORTRAN and COBOL (e.g., ANSI and CODASYL) are aware of the problems. At some point in the next five years, we will probably have much-improved versions of these two most-common languages. COBOL, for example, will probably have a DO-WHILE (for in-line loops), a CASE, and an END-IF by the early 1980's.

2. In the meantime, most of the ugly features of a programming language can be hidden by a *preprocessor*. One of the most popular COBOL preprocessors is ADR's METACOBOL, which provides the appropriate structuring verbs. There are literally dozens of cheap, available FORTRAN structuring preprocessors. The September 1975 issue of *ACM SIGPLAN Notices* contains a survey of approximately 20 preprocessors.

5.2.4 Programmers' ignorance of their programming language

As we observed in the previous section, the popular high-level programming languages lack some of the features that would make structured programming convenient. However, there is a much worse problem: Many programmers are ignorant of the language features that one must use to write structured code!

There is a certain irony to this -- particularly with PL/I. As we discussed earlier, PL/I is probably the most suitable of the popular high-level languages, for it has a DO-WHILE, an IF-THEN-ELSE, and various other powerful features. Most people (especially COBOL programmers!) assume that, since PL/I is a powerful language, PL/I programmers must be powerful people. That is, almost everyone *assumes* that PL/I programmers write good structured code -- because, after all, their language makes it so *easy*!

The trouble is that many PL/I programmers have *never* used a DO-WHILE statement, and have no idea how it works. Many of them have *never* used a nested IF statement, and have used a simple IF-THEN-ELSE only on rare occasions. Many of them, you see, are still writing a disguised form of FORTRAN (or COBOL, or RPG, or assembly language) in PL/I. A survey of more than 100 commercial applications in one of my clients' organizations showed that, in 100,000 lines of PL/I code, there were only 11 DO-WHILE statements -- and that in approximately 20% of the programs, there were *no* IF-THEN-ELSE statements.

Things are not much better in the COBOL world. Most of the COBOL programmers I encounter have *never* used a CALL statement, except possibly to CALL a data base management function provided by their vendor. Most of them have never used a nested IF statement, and the majority really don't understand how a simple IF-THEN-ELSE works. Most of them have never used the PERFORM-UNTIL statement, and are extremely cautious about using the special iterative case, PERFORM-VARYING. Only a very few COBOL programmers have any concept of a block structure -- that is, the concept of a group of statements that can be treated as if they were a "block," an integral unit.

So, what should we do? Shoot all of our existing programmers and get some new ones? The idea is tempting -- particularly since he better universities are teaching beginners how to use those features of their language that they *need* to know in order to write structured programs.

Shooting your existing programmers is messy and expensive (and possibly illegal) ... but the comment above indicates what the real problem is: training. The reason most PL/I programmers don't know how to use a DO-WHILE statement is that nobody ever taught them how -- and nobody ever suggested that it would be a good idea to use such features of their language.* Similarly in COBOL, nobody taught most COBOL programmers how to use PERFORM-UNTIL, or IF-THEN-ELSE, or any of the other structured aspects of their language.

So, if you want your programmers to write good structured code, it may be wise to send them back to school to brush up on some of the fundamentals of their language. It should only take a day or two of their time, and the effort will be repaid many times over.

5.2.5 Difficulty applying structured programming in assembly language

The reaction of an assembly language programmer to structured programming is fairly predictable: "What does all of this have to do with me? How can I possibly eliminate GOTO statements in an assembly language program? Everyone knows that assembly language programs have got to jump around!"

To answer this, we retreat to the original Böhm and Jacopini work. *Any* procedural logic can be flowcharted in a structured fashion, as a combination of "one-in-one-out" blocks of logic. That statement is true regardless of whether we are flowcharting the logic for a payroll system, or order entry system, a compiler, a real-time operating system, or anything else. And it is true whether that logic is eventually coded in COBOL, ALGOL, or assembly language.

The nice thing about COBOL, ALGOL, and the high-level languages is that they accept the structured flowcharts that we showed in Figure 5.1 *directly*. In assembly language, we have to hand-compile our structured flowcharts into the primitive instructions that make the machine work.

So, our answer to the assembly language programmer is, "Yes, you have to use branching instructions in your program. But your code should be a direct implementation of well-structured flowcharts; your code should consist of blocks with one entry and one exit."

---

*This is particularly true in PL/I. My same client who found that virtually none of their programmers used a DO-WHILE also found that 50% of the verbs in the PL/I language had essentially *never* been used. PL/I is such a rich language that most programmers learn only the subset that they need to get along....

In addition, we can offer the following suggestions about writing structured programs in assembly language:

1. If your programmers are working on a large machine (e.g., an IBM System/370) or on a small machine with a powerful macro assembler, you may want to consider using macros to implement DO-WHILE, IF-THEN-ELSE, etc. There are several standard packages of such macros available on IBM computers, and your programmers should be ingenious enough to develop them on other computers -- *if* the computer has a decent macro assembler (which many minicomputers don't!).

2. You may want to consider a preprocessor that gives you the ability to write IF-THEN-ELSE and DO-WHILE statements intermingled with "ordinary" assembler statements. This might be useful if your vendor's assembler doesn't have a macro capability.

3. You may want to pester your vendor to see if he has a so-called systems implementation language that you can use. IBM's PL/S language is a good example of this. Alternatively, you might consider PL/360 -- which was described in detail by Niklaus Wirth in the January 1968 issue of *The Journal of the ACM*. Many of the DEC computers will execute a language called BLISS; Control Data has a language called SWL (Software Writer's Language); and so forth. These languages generally provide the structuring verbs, *plus* powerful means of representing data, *plus* the normal assembly language instructions.

4. You may want to require your programmers to describe their procedural logic in a pseudocode -- i.e., something that resembles an informal mixture of English, ALGOL, PL/I, and FORTRAN, *but is structured*. This pseudocode expression of their logic can serve as a comment preceding the assembly language implementation. Pseudocode comments may also be placed in the comment field beside each assembly language instruction, but my experience has been that programmers won't maintain these comments as the code is modified in the maintenance phase of the project.

5. Finally, you may decide to ignore structured programming in an assembly language environment. Put your energy into structured design: Make sure that your programmers have designed their system in terms of small (less than 50 statements) modules that are highly cohesive and independent of other modules. If they do their job well in this area, what their code looks like won't matter so much -- *although there should never be any excuse for disorganized code.*

5.2.6 Attitude problems with "old-timers"

We discussed most of the common attitude problems in Chapter 2 of this book. Thus, I need only remind you here that you *will* encounter some emotional objections -- mostly from programmers who have been coding for ten years without ever being told *how* to code.

As a manager, you should be able to respond to the following kind of comments:

- "You're limiting my creativity."
- "My old way works fine."
- "Are you trying to tell me that I've been writing bad programs all these years?"
- "Are you trying to tell me that *you* know how to write programs better than I do -- I started programming while you were still in diapers!"
- "It's a great idea, but it'll never work on our system."
- "I don't see what difference structured programming will make."

We should also observe that many of the negative reactions to structured programming have occurred in organizations that enforced "GOTO-less" programming with a religious fervor. If you're prepared to let your programmers stick an occasional GOTO into their code -- particularly to compensate for limitations in their programming language -- chances are they won't squawk quite so loudly.

5.2.7 Complaints of inefficiency

Most of the complaints here are similar -- if not identical -- to the complaints about the inefficiency of structured design. And most of our answers should be the same, too! Rather than repeating the philosophical points in Section 4.2.5, I'll mention only a few points that are pertinent to structured programming.

Why do programmers think that structured programming is inefficient? There seem to be a few consistent arguments:

1. The IF-THEN-ELSE statement occasionally generates somewhat less efficient code than the programmer could have written with GOTO statements. Several years ago, the difference in efficiency was significant -- often a factor of two or more. Today, the programmer can assume that *at worst* the IF-THEN-ELSE statement might cost him a microsecond or two, and possibly an extra byte of storage.

2. A "religious" interpretation of structured programming often leads to a few extra flags and switches (mostly so the programmer can exit from the middle of a loop). That may cost him a microsecond or two.

3. In a few cases, structured programming requires the programmer to duplicate small blocks of code -- rather than using a GOTO to jump into the code from several different places. This may make the program slightly larger than it would otherwise have been.

In almost all cases, we are talking about microseconds of inefficiency -- whereas the *real* questions of efficiency involve *hours* of computer time, and can only be achieved by intelligent systems design.

5.2.8 Conflicts with old programming standards

Another potential problem you'll face is that the techniques of structured programming may conflict with your current programming standards. For example -- and this is probably *the* most common example -- many programming standards forbid (or strongly discourage) nested IF statements.

So, what should we do? From a slightly cynical point of view, I suggest that you really don't have a problem -- since most of your programmers don't really read the standards manual anyway! In many cases, the only reason they raise the issue is to find some excuse for not using structured programming.

Seriously, it's usually a simple matter to change the standards manual to conform with structured programming. Indeed, it may require only that you pull out the section that tells the programmer not to use nested IF statements. A more serious problem is that your standards manual may have several examples of supposedly good code -- all of which are unstructured!

We will discuss the whole question of standards in Chapter 12. In the meantime, you may wish to examine the programming standards we've developed at YOURDON inc. for COBOL, which can be found in the appendix.

5.2.9 Difficulty enforcing structured programming standards

Another objection is often raised at this point. "Assuming that we develop structured programming standards, how do we enforce them? How do we ensure that a programmer uses a GOTO statement only when he has to?"

If, as a manager, you wish to enforce "religious" standards, there is a simple answer to all of this: Build a "standards-enforcer" package and *insist* that all new programs be run through the package before being put into production. That way, you can ensure that nobody uses any GOTO statements (if that's what you want), that nobody has more than three levels of nested IF statements (if that's what you want), and that everyone has followed whatever other standards you've decided to enforce.

I am not aware of *any* companies that are doing this (although there may be some). Most organizations have "soft" standards -- or guidelines -- which are to be interpreted by the programmer with a certain degree of common sense. Thus, we normally see standards like, "Don't use GOTO statements unless you have to, or unless you honestly think that the code would be more understandable."

How do we ensure that standards of this type are put into practice? There's a very simple answer: Use structured walkthroughs, or team programming. If the team thinks that the code is good code, then it probably *is* good code, whether or not it has GOTO statements.

Walkthroughs are discussed in considerably more detail in Chapter 9.

5.2.10 Difficulty using structured programming in a maintenance environment

We observed in Chapter 2 that 50% (or more) of the effort in many organizations today is *maintenance* -- patching and correcting and improving existing programs. Most, if not all, of these programs were written in an unstructured fashion. So what relevance does structured programming have in an environment like this?

Unfortunately, there are no magic answers to this problem. One can make a few common-sense suggestions: For example, the advantages of structured programming may influence an organization to rewrite an old application sooner than would have been politically possible otherwise. Also: If large "chunks" of code are to be changed or inserted into an existing program, it should be possible to do such work in a structured fashion.

A few organizations have toyed with the idea of a structuring engine" -- i.e., a package that automatically converts an unstructured program into an equivalent structured program. Such an engine is theoretically possible (indeed, the original Böhm and Jacopini paper suggested the outlines of such an engine), and at least one software firm has actually developed such a package. However, there are some problems that should be kept in mind:

1. After five or ten years of maintaining some rotten old program, your maintenance programmers may finally have gotten to the point where they *understand* it. A structuring engine would rearrange the code to the point where they probably wouldn't understand it any more....

2. A structuring engine is usually based on the assumption that the program obeys the legal syntax of the language. This is not always true, particularly in COBOL: Programmers have a way of using undocumented, illegal features of the language that shouldn't work, but *do*. A structuring engine would upset this delicate balance.

3. A structuring engine cannot transmute lead into gold: It cannot convert a truly bad program into a truly good program. It *can* eliminate the GOTO statements, and it may improve the organization of the procedural logic ... but there is always the chance that it will do nothing more than transform a bad unstructured program into an equally bad structured program.

There is also another problem that you should anticipate: If you teach your programmers all about structured programming, they will become *very* frustrated if they are sent back to the maintenance department to continue patching unstructured "rat's-nest" code. It might be safer to leave your maintenance programmers in the dark -- don't teach them anything about structured programming....

But that leads to another problem: The first time your maintenance programmers are given a *structured* program to maintain, they'll probably have a nervous fit. "What's this?" they'll say. "Nested IF statements? I've never seen such things! And subroutine calls? My God!! I can't read any of this!" Perhaps you should teach them something about structured programming after all.

Keep one other thing in mind: The *first few structured* programs written by your development programmers actually may be a little difficult to maintain. As we suggested earlier, a structured GOTO-less program is not necessarily a *good* program -- and until your programmers really know what they're doing, they actually may write some *bad* structured code. Your maintenance programmers will certainly let you know if that's the case -- and you should listen to them.

5.2.11 Difficulties with nested IF statement

The last problem area that we discuss in this chapter is perhaps the most pervasive one: Programmers seem to have great difficulty writing code of the following form:

```
IF MARITAL-STATUS = MARRIED
     THEN IF SEX = MALE
          THEN IF AGE GREATER THAN 30
               BLAH
               BLAH
               BLAH
          ELSE
               BLAH
               BLAH
     ELSE
          IF AGE GREATER THAN 45
               BLAH
               BLAH
          ELSE
               BLAH
               BLAH
ELSE IF MARITAL-STATUS = SINGLE
     ETC.
```

This kind of code is known as a "nested IF." Don't worry if you find it a little difficult to understand -- your programmers do, too!

Why is the issue of nested IF statements associated with structured programming? Simply because the GOTO statement has been taken away! Previously, your programmers would have written code like the following:

```
IF MARITAL-STATUS = MARRIED AND SEX = MALE AND
     AGE GREATER THAN 30 GO TO X-ROUTINE
ELSE GO TO Y-ROUTINE.
```

Without his GOTO statement, the programmer finds that he is coding more and more IF-THEN-ELSE statements nested inside other IF-THEN-ELSE statements.

Without getting too deeply into technical issues, I would like to offer the following suggestions:

1. Many of the problems here are *training* problems, as we observed in Section 5.2.4. Most of your programmers have never been taught how the IF-THEN-ELSE statement works. Give your programmers a little "refresher" seminar, and most of your problems will go away.

2. Some of the problems are attitude problems: Some programmers just don't like the ELSE statement. "What's wrong with the GOTO to get out of the middle of a nested IF?" they'll say. "I've been doing it for years, and it works just fine." This is one area where you may decide to back off from the religious interpretation of GOTO-less programming, and let them do what they want. Make sure, though, that they know what they're doing, and that they are using the GOTO statement because they honestly, sincerely believe the code is easier to read. Many programmers who use this argument don't want to admit that they haven't figured out how to eliminate their GOTO's.

3. Many programmers confuse nested IF statements with something quite different: compound Boolean conditional expressions. That is, you'll hear some programmers say, "I don't like nested IF statements because I always get into trouble with statements like this: IF X NOT EQUAL Y OR Z THEN GO TO AFGHANISTAN." True, that is a messy statement -- but it has nothing to do with the problem of nested IF statements. While you're giving your programmers a refresher course on nested IF's, though, you might also give them a short course on Boolean logic -- most programmers sorely need it!

4. Many programmers confuse nested IF's with so-called CASE structures. There are many situations, for example, where the programmer wants to write

```
IF MARITAL-STATUS = MARRIED
     BLAH
     BLAH
ELSE
     IF MARITAL-STATUS = SINGLE
          BLAH
          BLAH
     ELSE
          IF MARITAL-STATUS = DIVORCED
               BLAH
               BLAH
          ELSE
               IF MARITAL-STATUS = WIDOWED
                    BLAH
                    BLAH
               ELSE
                    PRINT AN ERROR MESSAGE.
```

The significant thing is that the example above is *not* a nested IF, but instead a simple "either-or" situation. Either a person is married, *or* single, *or* divorced, or... -- but only one! We should recognize this by writing

```
IF MARITAL-STATUS = MARRIED
    BLAH
    BLAH
ELSE IF MARITAL-STATUS = SINGLE
    BLAH
    BLAH
ELSE IF MARITAL-STATUS = DIVORCED
    BLAH
    BLAH
ELSE IF MARITAL-STATUS = WIDOWED
    BLAH
    BLAH
ELSE
    PRINT AN ERROR MESSAGE.
```

When it is written in this fashion, it becomes obvious that we could string *hundreds* of these ELSE-IF's together without making the code any more difficult to understand. The reason? Very simple: We only have to consider one IF at a time.

5. An occasional complaint about nested IF statements has to do with their formatting. Note how the first version of our MARITAL-STATUS example above was indented several spaces for each "level"; after five or six levels, we run out of room. As we implied, though, this is sometimes a false issue:

If the code is written in the ELSE-IF style shown in our second version; we should have no problem. If we have *real* nested IF statements (such as the one at the very beginning of this section), then we deserve to run out of room after five or six levels!

6. Programmers sometimes complain that it is difficult to understand more than a few levels of nested IF's. Indeed it is! Note that the problem is that of a human being trying to comprehend a difficult logical statement -- the issue is *not* whether the computer can understand a nested IF. Recognizing that the problem is a human one, we can draw on a wealth of experience and studies of human ability to understand complexity. These studies (carried out by people like Noam Chomsky in the field of linguistics, and Gerald Weinberg in the programming field) suggest that very few people can understand more than three levels of *real* nested IF's.

7. If the application *requires* more than three levels of nested decisions, then the programmer should break it into separate pieces (i.e., separate modules) which can be comprehended separately. Thus, the example at the beginning of this section might have been coded as

```
IF MARITAL-STATUS = MARRIED
      THEN IF SEX = MALE
           PERFORM MARRIED-MALE-ROUTINE
      ELSE
           ETC.
```

8. Finally: Many nested IF problems are an indication that the programmer is unfamiliar with decision tables. The code at the beginning of this section, for example, dealt with *at least* three different variables: marital status, sex, and age. If we wish to recognize five different kinds of marital status, then there are 5x2x2 different combinations of these three variables -- and whether the programmer uses GOTO statements or nested IF statements, he'd better make darn sure that he has considered all 20 different combinations! What leads to bugs is the common tendency to forget a few of those combinations, or the tendency to get them

mixed up -- and a decision table approach is probably the best way to (a) make sure that all combinations are expressed, (b) make sure that redundancies, ambiguities, and contradictions have been eliminated, and (c) organize the logic in such a way that it can be coded trivially. Ask your programmers to draw you a decision table for the MARITAL-STATUS problem -- and if they give you a blank look, send them back to school for *that* before you worry about nested IF statements!

Chapter 5: References

1. Baker, F.T., "Chief Programmer Team Management of Production Programming," *IBM Systems Journal*, January 1972. An account of IBM's first formal use of structured programming.

2. Baker, F.T., "System Quality Through Structured Programming," *Proceedings of the 1972 Fall Joint Computer Conference*, pages 339-342. A further account of The New York Times system, with statistics on the number of bugs found.

3. Böhm, C., and G. Jacopini, "Flow Diagrams, Turing Machines, and Languages with Only Two Formulation Rules," *Communications of the ACM*, May 1966, pages 366-371. This paper forms much of the theoretical basis for structured programming. Very theoretical and very hard to read -- and not really necessary for your application programmers. However, you should know that it exists.

4. Dahl, O.J., E.W. Dijkstra, and C.A.R. Hoare, *Structured Programming*, Prentice-Hall, 1972. One of the first -- if not *the* first -- books on structured programming. Also one of the more academic ones. Probably way over the head of the average COBOL, PL/I, and FORTRAN programmer, but exciting reading nonetheless.

5. Kernighan, B.W., and P.J. Plauger, *The Elements of Programming Style*, McGraw-Hill, 1974. An excellent book that emphasizes that the object of the game is not to just write structured programs -- but to write *good* programs.

6. Kernighan, B.W., and P.J. Plauger, *Software Tools*, Addison-Wesley, 1976. Another excellent book, this gives some 5,000 lines of real, working, structured code -- written in a language called RATFOR. RATFOR is one of the more popular structured preprocessors for FORTRAN.

7. Knuth, D.E., "Structured Programming with GOTO Statements," *ACM Computing Surveys*, December 1974, pages 261-302. A slightly different point of view from one of the best programmers in the world, the author of the formidable *The Art of Computer Programming*, Addison-Wesley, 1968.

8. McGowan, C.L., and J.R. Kelly, *Top-Down Structured Programming*, Petrocelli/Charter, 1975. Somewhat more oriented toward PL/I than the other high-level languages. Academic (discussions of proofs of program correctness, etc.) but still very useful for applications programmers.

9. Plauger, P.J., "New York Times Revisited," *The YOURDON Report*, Volume 1, Number 3, April 1976. A follow-up account of The New York Times system after several years of maintenance.

10. Weinberg, G., *Structured Programming in PL/C*, John Wiley & Sons, 1972. Another introductory book, this one using a subset of PL/I.

11. Yourdon, E., "A Brief Look at Structured Programming and Top-Down Design," *Modern Data*, June 1974, pages 30-35. A very brief overview, and not sufficient to get your programmers started actually writing structured code.

12. Yourdon, E., C. Gane, and T. Sarson, *Learning to Program in Structured COBOL*, YOURDON inc., 1976. Just what the title implies: a book for COBOL beginners.

13. Yourdon, E., *Techniques of Program Structure and Design*, Prentice-Hall, 1975. Aimed at experienced programmers, one chapter is exclusively devoted to structured programming.

Chapter 6 HOW TO MANAGE DOCUMENTATION FOR THE NEW PPT TECHNIQUES

At this point, we have discussed the most important *technical* aspects of the PPT techniques: top-down design, top-down implementation, structured design, and structured programming. Now we are ready to discuss the problems of *documenting* EDP systems that are produced by these techniques.

You may have noticed that there were very few illustrations -- particularly technical diagrams -- in the previous chapters. Chapter 4 contained a few "company organization charts" to illustrate the concept of span of control, and Chapter 5 contained a few conventional flowcharts to illustrate the basic elements of structured programming. To a large extent, this paucity of illustrations was intentional: I feel it is important that the technical concepts of design and programming be understood first, so that the discussion of documentation can build from it.

A documentation technique is a documentation technique -- and it should not be confused with the concepts of design that we discussed in previous chapters. A flowchart is only a picture; the act of drawing a flowchart does not ensure a good design. Unfortunately, I have seen many organizations confuse this point: When asked whether they are practicing structured design, such organizations say, "Sure! We *must* be doing structured design -- after all, we're drawing HIPO diagrams and a bunch of other funny-looking things that we never did before!"

HIPO? What's that? Indeed, what *kind* of documentation are we talking about? I think it is practical to organize the incredible mass of documentation that accompanies most EDP development projects into three categories:

- documentation that is normally associated with systems analysis
- documentation that describes the *structural* design of a system
- documentation that describes and illustrates the *procedural* design of an individual module of the system -- e.g., documentation of the sort provided by detailed flowcharts

Some of this documentation will not be influenced by the PPT techniques. That is, it is likely that you will continue documenting your systems as you always have -- *to some extent.* However, the PPT techniques will probably introduce some new documentation techniques in your organization -- and may cause you to abandon certain other techniques.

My purpose in this chapter is to discuss the impact of the PPT techniques in each of the three areas of documentation listed above. In keeping with the theme of the previous three chapters, I will also discuss the problems you, as a manager, are likely to have in your attempt to implement some of the new techniques.

For reasons that will not be clear until later in the chapter, I will begin with a discussion of documentation techniques to illustrate the structural design of a system.

6.1 Documentation to Illustrate the Structural Design of a System

The basic point I would like to make here is that many organizations have *no* structural documentation techniques. They have narrative specifications, they have flowcharts, and they have various other bits and pieces of paper. But in most cases, these classical forms of documentation do very little to illustrate the *structure* and *architecture* of a system.

Because of this, some new documentation techniques -- introduced originally to illustrate the structured design concepts in Chapter 4 -- have had a profound impact on some organizations. For the first time, designer/programmers have been able to *see* the system architectures they have been designing blindly for years; and merely *seeing* what they are doing has often been sufficient for them to make substantial improvements in the quality of their design.

The three most important documentation techniques in this area are

- o the data flow diagram
- o the HIPO hierarchy chart
- o the structure chart

We will discuss each of these techniques separately.

6.1.1 The data flow diagram

The *data flow diagram* is also known as a "program graph," or a "bubble chart"; its purpose is to show the flow of data through a large program or system. A typical data flow diagram is shown in Figure 6.1. If the diagram looks alien, perhaps I can reassure you by pointing out that Figure 6.1 is identical to the conventional "system flowchart" that your programmers have traditionally drawn for your EDP systems -- except that it does not indicate whether the processing activities will be implemented as "modules," or "programs," or "job steps," or "minicomputers," or some other physical form. Similarly, Figure 6.1 does not indicate whether the data that flows between

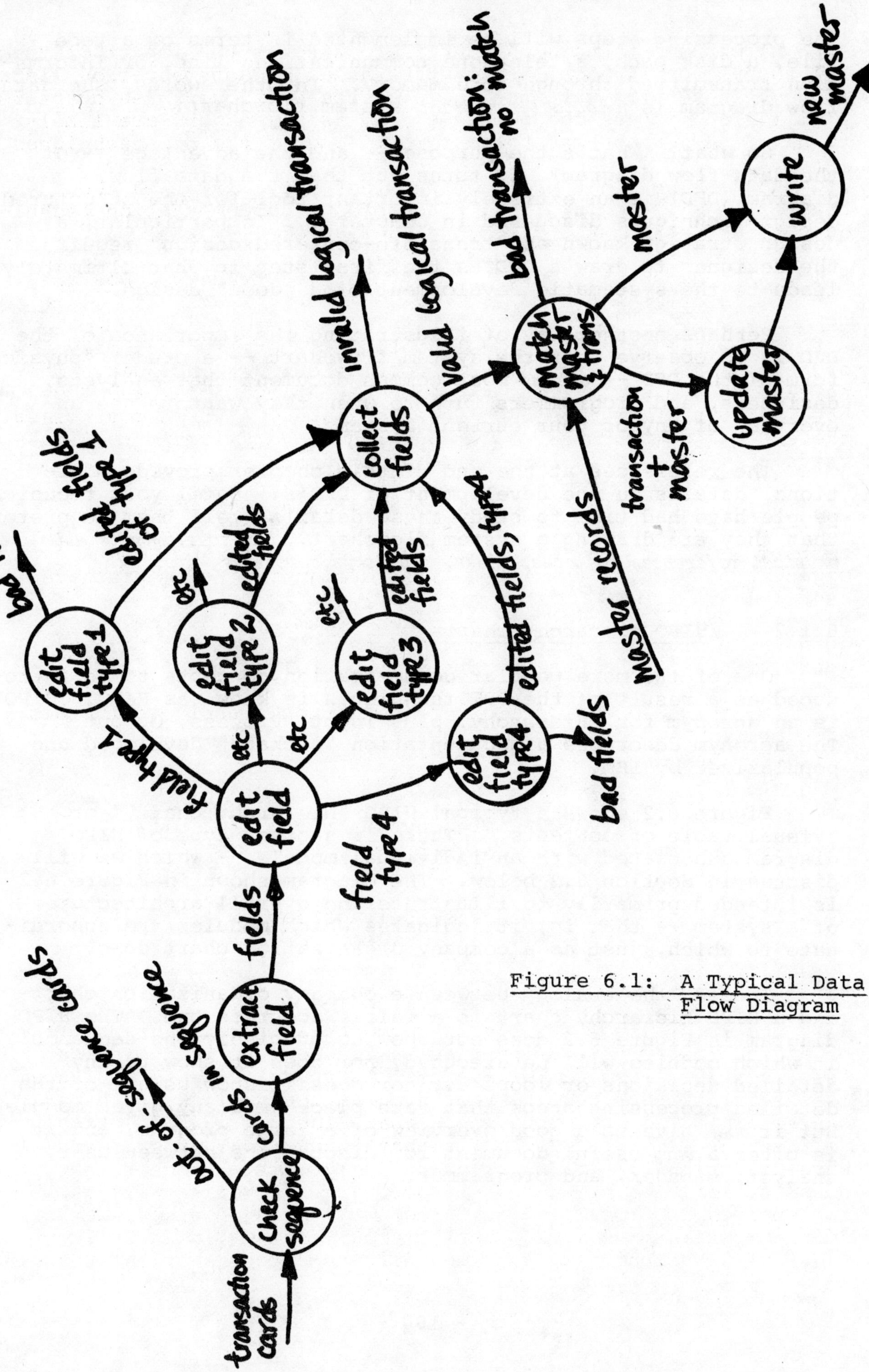

Figure 6.1: A Typical Data Flow Diagram

the processing steps will be implemented in terms of a tape file, a disk pack, a telephone communications line, or information transmitted through core memory. In other words, the data flow diagram is a *logical, abstract* system flowchart.

So what? What's the purpose -- and the advantage -- of the data flow diagram? It turns out that the data flow diagram (DFD) is an extremely important tool for the structured design techniques discussed in Chapter 4. In particular, a design strategy known as "transform-centered design" requires the designer to draw a DFD as the first step in what ultimately leads to the systematic development of a "good" design.

Perhaps another way of illustrating the importance of the DFD is to observe that the system flowchart -- a crude, "physical" form of the DFD -- is *the* most common document that analysts, designers, and programmers turn to when they want to see an overview of any of your current systems.

The references at the end of this chapter provide additional details on the development of DFD's. Until your technical people have had time to study these details, tell them to pretend that they are drawing a system flowchart, *but to eliminate all physical references to tapes, disks, job steps, programs, etc.*

6.1.2 HIPO hierarchy charts

One of the more popular documentation concepts to be introduced as a result of the PPT techniques is known as HIPO. HIPO is an acronym for "Hierarchy, plus Input, Process, Output." The acronym describes a documentation "package" developed and popularized by IBM.

Figure 6.2 shows a typical HIPO "hierarchy chart," or "visual table of contents." There is another type of HIPO diagram associated with an individual module -- which we will discuss in Section 6.2 below. The diagram shown in Figure 6.2 is intended primarily to illustrate the overall architecture of a system -- that is, it indicates which modules are subordinate to which, just as a company organization chart does.

Indeed, the analogy between a company organization chart and a HIPO hierarchy chart is a fairly accurate one. The HIPO diagram in Figure 6.2 does not show us precisely the sequence in which modules will be executed, nor does it show us any detailed decisions or loops ... nor does it show us any of the detailed processing steps that take place *inside* any given module. But it *does* give us a good overview of a large program, and it is often a *very* useful document for discussions between user, analyst, manager, and programmer.

Figure 6.2

A typical HIPO hierarchy chart

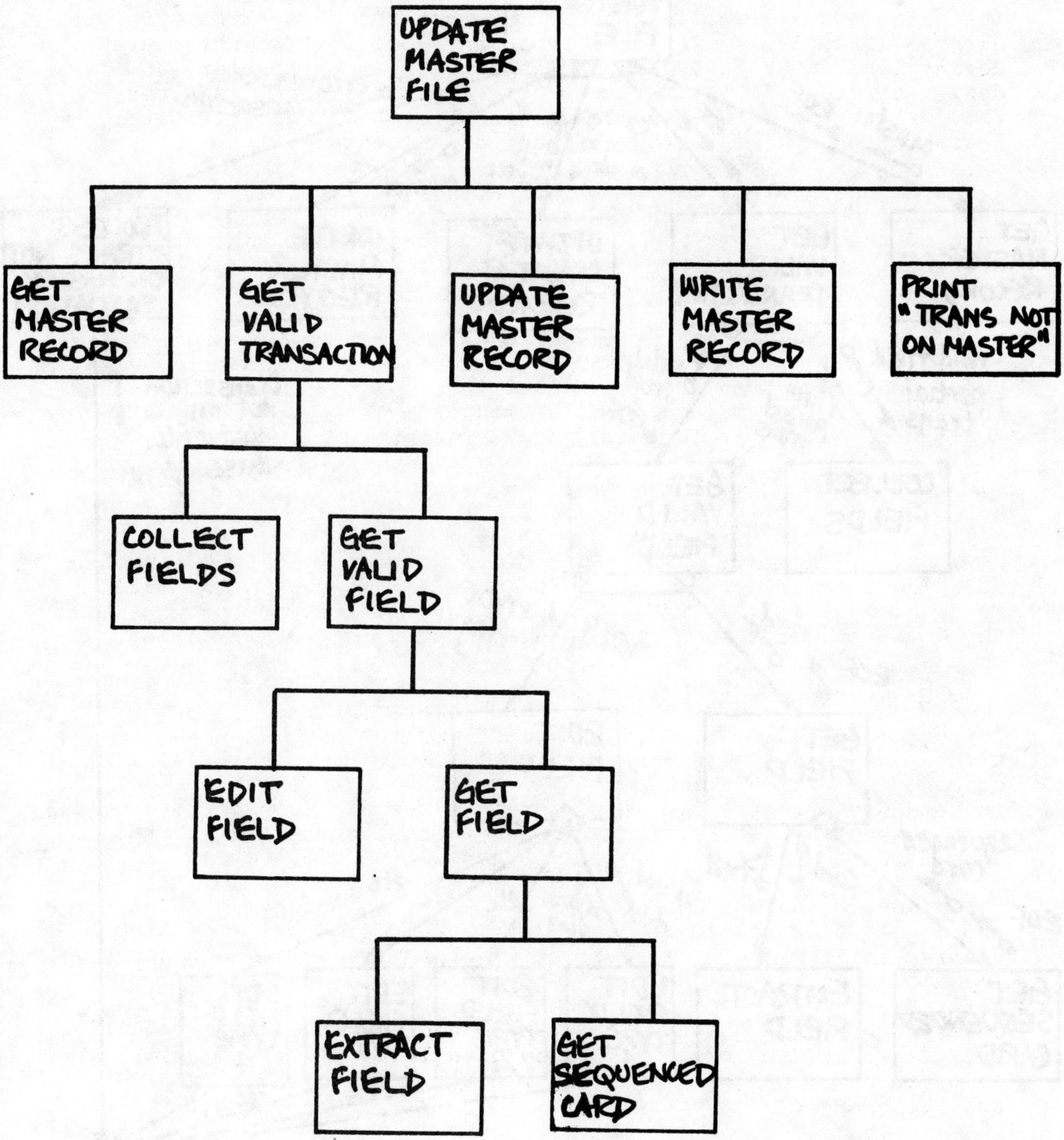

Figure 6.3: A typical structure chart.

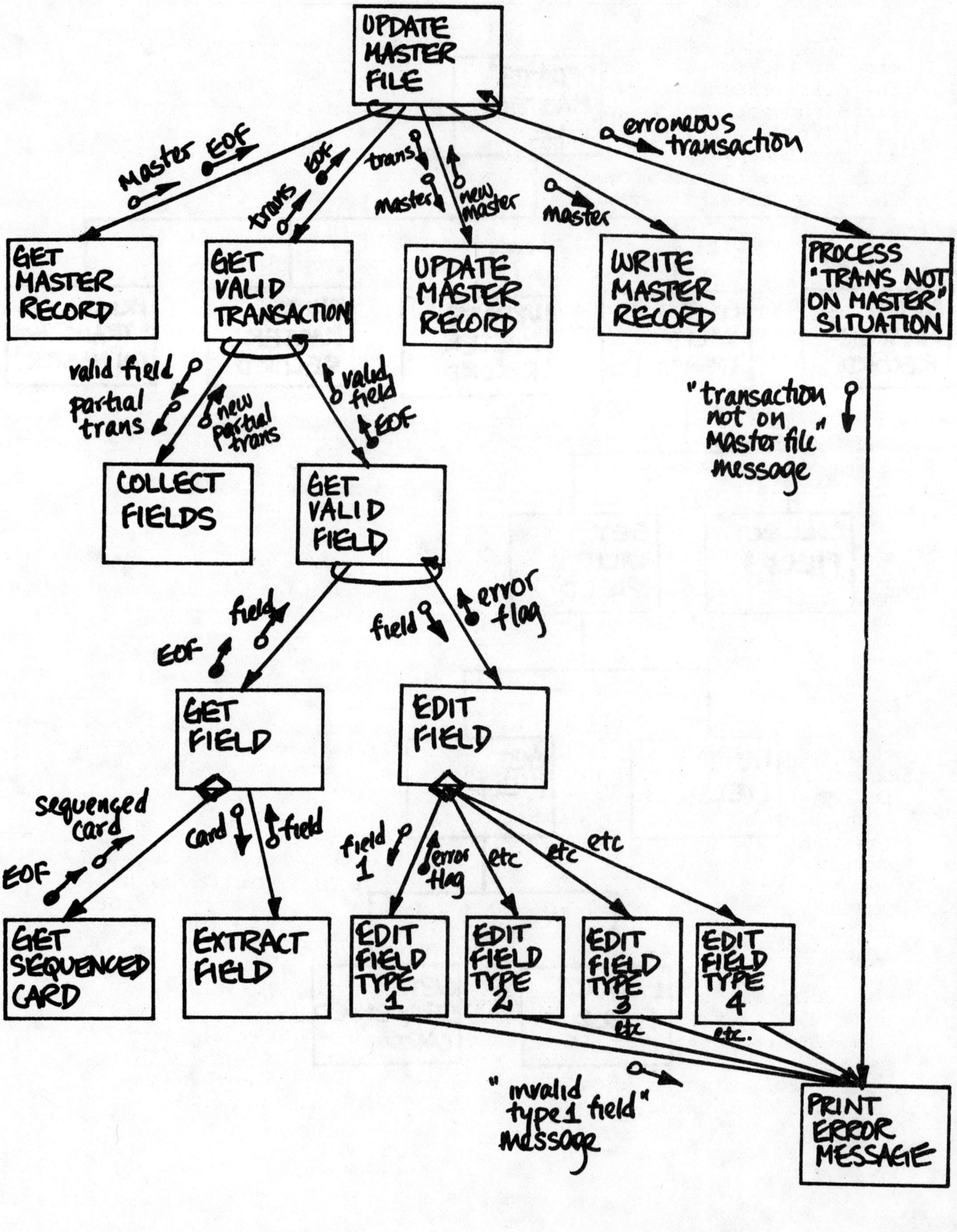

6.1.3 Structure charts

A variation on the HIPO hierarchy chart is known as a "structure chart" -- an example of which is given in Figure 6.3.

To a large extent, the structure chart conveys the same kind of information as the HIPO chart of Figure 6.2 -- many of the differences are cosmetic. Note, for example, that the lines connecting the various modules in Figure 6.3 are drawn in a "tree-structured" fashion, rather than the horizontal and vertical lines that characterize Figure 6.2. Note also that the connecting lines terminate in an arrowhead, whereas the lines in a HIPO diagram do *not* terminate in an arrowhead.

A slightly more significant aspect of the structure chart is its ability to show some occasional *procedural* detail, without getting bogged down in detail. Figure 6.3 shows the presence of *some* loops and *some* decisions that the designer felt were sufficiently important to be shown. Such procedural details *could* be included with HIPO, too -- but the "official" version of HIPO does *not* include this information.

Perhaps the most significant aspect of the structure chart is that it shows the interfaces between the modules -- *on the structure chart itself*. That is, Figure 6.3 shows the inputs and outputs associated with all of the modules.

By contrast, the HIPO hierarchy chart of Figure 6.2 does *not* show the interfaces between the modules. Some organizations suggest the use of an "input-output table" -- a separate document that lists, in a tabular fashion, each module's inputs and outputs. Other organizations suggest that such details be shown on the document that describes the individual modules -- i.e., on the "detail" HIPO diagram that we will discuss in Section 6.2.

Significantly, though, many organizations do not realize that this is an issue at all. That is, they draw HIPO hierarchy charts, as in Figure 6.2, and *never* bother to think about the interfaces, until they get around to writing the code. Even then, they may not think about the interfaces in a formal fashion: *All* of the system's data may be defined in, and available from, the DATA DIVISION of a COBOL program (or equivalent forms of global data in other programs -- e.g., blank COMMON in FORTRAN). As a result, the interfaces are often not defined in a formal manner -- they just "evolve" as the code is written.

A number of organizations have found it advantageous to show the intermodule interfaces on the same diagram -- on the same sheet of paper -- as the hierarchical "picture" of the system. There is, of course, the danger that this extra information will clutter up the diagram to the point where it is unreadable; however, we make the following observations:

- The designer records the highest level *aggregate* of data being passed between two modules. That is, if module A passes a master-file record to module B, we simply write "master record" on the structure chart -- we do not write the names of all 178 fields in the master record.

- If the diagram becomes cluttered, it is often an indication that the design could be improved. That is, one of the signs of a "good" design is a clean set of interfaces, with relatively few distinct forms of data being passed between modules.

- In fact, those organizations who have drawn structure charts of the form shown in Figure 6.3 have generally found that the diagram is *not* cluttered with too much detail. To borrow from an old television commercial: Try it, you'll like it!

6.2 Documentation to Illustrate the Procedural Design of a System

The documentation techniques discussed in the previous section are useful for illustrating the overall structure of a system -- but they give little or no information about the detailed procedural design of each module. So, this leads us to ask: What impact have the PPT techniques had on *detailed* documentation?

For a few organizations, nothing has changed. The programmers still write detailed flowcharts and detailed narrative specifications of each module. Serious efforts are made to keep this documentation up-to-date during the maintenance phase of the project, and the maintenance programmer has some feeling of confidence that the flowcharts bear some resemblance to the code that he is maintaining.

It is safe to say, however, that not *many* organizations are continuing to work in this fashion. Management standards, contractual obligations, and other external pressures may dictate that the detailed flowcharts be produced -- but they rarely are useful. In most organizations, the programmers will tell you that (a) they never draw the flowchart until *after* the program is working (making it probable that the flowchart indicates what the programmer *thinks* his code is doing rather than what his code really *is* doing); (b) flowcharts are not kept up-to-date during the maintenance effort, because it's too much of a hassle; and (c) as a result of (b), the maintenance programmers know that they're wasting their time if they bother looking at the flowcharts.

One of the interesting results of the PPT techniques is that some organizations have finally *admitted* this reality to themselves. Why this discovery had to wait for the introduction of structured programming, I don't know -- but I *do* know that the introduction of structured programming has caused some organizations to abandon detailed flowcharts completely.

If one abandons detailed flowcharts, what does one substitute in their place? For some organizations, the answer is: *nothing*. The logic is very simple: The structure charts or HIPO hierarchy charts provide an overall picture of the system. If the design has been done according to the principles of structured design, it should be possible for the maintenance programmer to maintain or debug one module without having to know anything about the detailed contents of any other module. If the code has been written according to the principles of structured programming, it should be possible to read the code without any comments. In this context, one could view a comment as an apology for bad code. In any case, there is no point maintaining the fiction that the detailed flowcharts are accurate -- better to have no documentation than incorrect documentation that breeds a sense of false security.

Even though such an argument may make eminently good sense, it is still considered somewhat radical. A substantial number of the EDP organizations that I come into contact with still require some level of detailed "design documentation" before the programmer is allowed to write the code -- and that documentation may well be kept for the benefit of the maintenance programmer.

For those who wish to continue some degree of detailed documentation -- but who are disillusioned with detailed flowcharts -- what techniques are available? It appears that three different types of documentation techniques have gained popularity in this area:

- pseudocode
- detailed HIPO diagrams
- Nassi-Schneiderman charts

Each of these techniques is discussed below.

6.2.1 Pseudocode

Pseudocode is also referred to as "structured English," "computer Esperanto," or any of a variety of other terms. Pseudocode could be defined as "narrative documentation" constructed from combinations of:

- simple, imperative English sentences containing a single, transitive verb and a single, non-plural object

- IF-THEN-ELSE constructs, of the sort discussed in Chapter 5

- DO-WHILE constructs of the sort discussed in Chapter 5

- other appropriate "extensions" to structured programming, such as CASE, REPEAT-UNTIL, etc.

An example of pseudocode is shown in Figure 6.4. It illustrates, I think, a general characteristic of pseudocode: It is reasonably well-organized and precise, and yet informal enough to be intelligible to non-programmers. And since it does not require a flowcharting template, pseudocode can be written quickly and easily -- and kept up-to-date more easily than a detailed flowchart or HIPO diagram (which means that there is more of a chance that it *will* be kept up-to-date).

Organizations that code in ALGOL, PL/I, or other powerful high-level languages often remark that the pseudocode is so close to the "real" code that it is a waste of time to bother with it; however, it is worth keeping in mind that a human reader does not require the same degree of precision as a compiler -- pseudocode seems to represent a nice compromise between precision and informality. Those who program in COBOL have mixed opinions on the usefulness of pseudocode: On the one hand, pseudocode is sufficiently close to "real" COBOL that one wonders whether it provides any useful information at all; on the other hand, pseudocode does afford the programmer the opportunity to express some structured logic that is *not* "natural" in COBOL -- e.g., logic expressed in terms of REPEAT-UNTIL's, CASE's, and other structured constructs.

In FORTRAN, BASIC, and assembly language (and other primitive languages of that sort), there is no question that pseudocode is of value. First, it allows the programmer to *think* in a structured fashion (which his "real" language does not allow him to do). Second, it provides a convenient basis for hand-compiling the "real" FORTRAN code (or assembly language code, etc.) in an almost mechanical fashion. And third, it provides an easy-to-read overview of the procedural logic for the maintenance programmer.

We must admit that some of the concerns about detailed flowcharts are still valid with pseudocode. How does the maintenance programmer know whether the pseudocode approximates the real code? How can we ensure that the pseudocode is updated whenever the real code is updated? The only argument I can give is that if pseudocode is easier to write, maintain,

Figure 6.4: An example of pseudocode.

```
MASTER-FILE-UPDATE:

  1. DO WHILE there are more transactions or there are more master records.

     a. IF the master account number is equal to the transaction account number:

        1. Update the master record from the transaction record.

        2. Write the updated master record.

        3. Get the next valid transaction record.

        4. Get the next master record.

     b. ELSE:

        1. IF the master account number is less than the transaction account number:

           a. Write the master record.

           b. Get the next master record.

        2. ELSE:

           a. Print an error message.

           b. Get the next valid transaction.

  2. Close the transaction file.

  3. Close the master file.
```

and update, it is *more likely* to be kept accurate and up-to-date than flowcharts. But there are no guarantees....

6.2.2 Detailed HIPO diagrams

Another "new" form of detailed documentation is known as a "detailed HIPO diagram," a "functional HIPO diagram," or an "IPO diagram." An example of a detailed HIPO diagram is given in Figure 6.5; note that this diagram can be cross-referenced to the HIPO hierarchy chart in Figure 6.2.

What can one say about detailed HIPO diagrams? Perhaps most important is that they show the relationships between module inputs, module processing logic, and module outputs in a highly graphic way. That feature is both a blessing and a curse. Because the information *is* presented in such a graphic fashion, it can be used as a means of conveying information to users, management, analysts, and programmers. On the other hand, because it *is* a graphic technique (as evidenced by the fact that IBM provides HIPO templates, HIPO coding pads, and a detailed manual on how to use HIPO -- much of which is devoted to a discussion of techniques for drawing the "fat" arrows in Figure 6.5 in such a way that they don't cross), it requires a non-trivial amount of artwork. And this leads to an obvious question: What are the chances that a detailed HIPO diagram will be updated if there is a change to the module at 3 in the morning? Indeed, what are the chances that the "real" code *ever* bears any resemblance to the detailed HIPO diagram? There is a good chance that the programmer (a) put considerable time and effort into his detailed HIPO diagram, (b) found, in the midst of writing the code, that he had to change some aspect of the procedural design, and (c) conveniently "forgot" to redraw his detailed HIPO diagram.

Thus, there is a serious concern that detailed HIPO diagrams will degenerate and decay in the same manner as detailed flowcharts. A few organizations have already abandoned detailed HIPO diagrams for just that reason.

A final observation is in order. Note that the central "process" portion of the detailed HIPO diagram is essentially the same as the pseudocode we discussed earlier. And note that the information shown in the "input" portion and the "output" portion of the detailed HIPO diagram *could* be shown (and, in my opinion, *should* be shown) on the "hierarchy chart" or "structure chart" that we discussed in Section 6.1. Thus, we end up with the impression that there is nothing really essential in the detailed HIPO diagram that could not be obtained with other techniques -- and the extra artwork involved in detailed HIPO diagrams poses some serious questions of maintenance.

Figure 6.5: A typical detailed HIPO diagram.

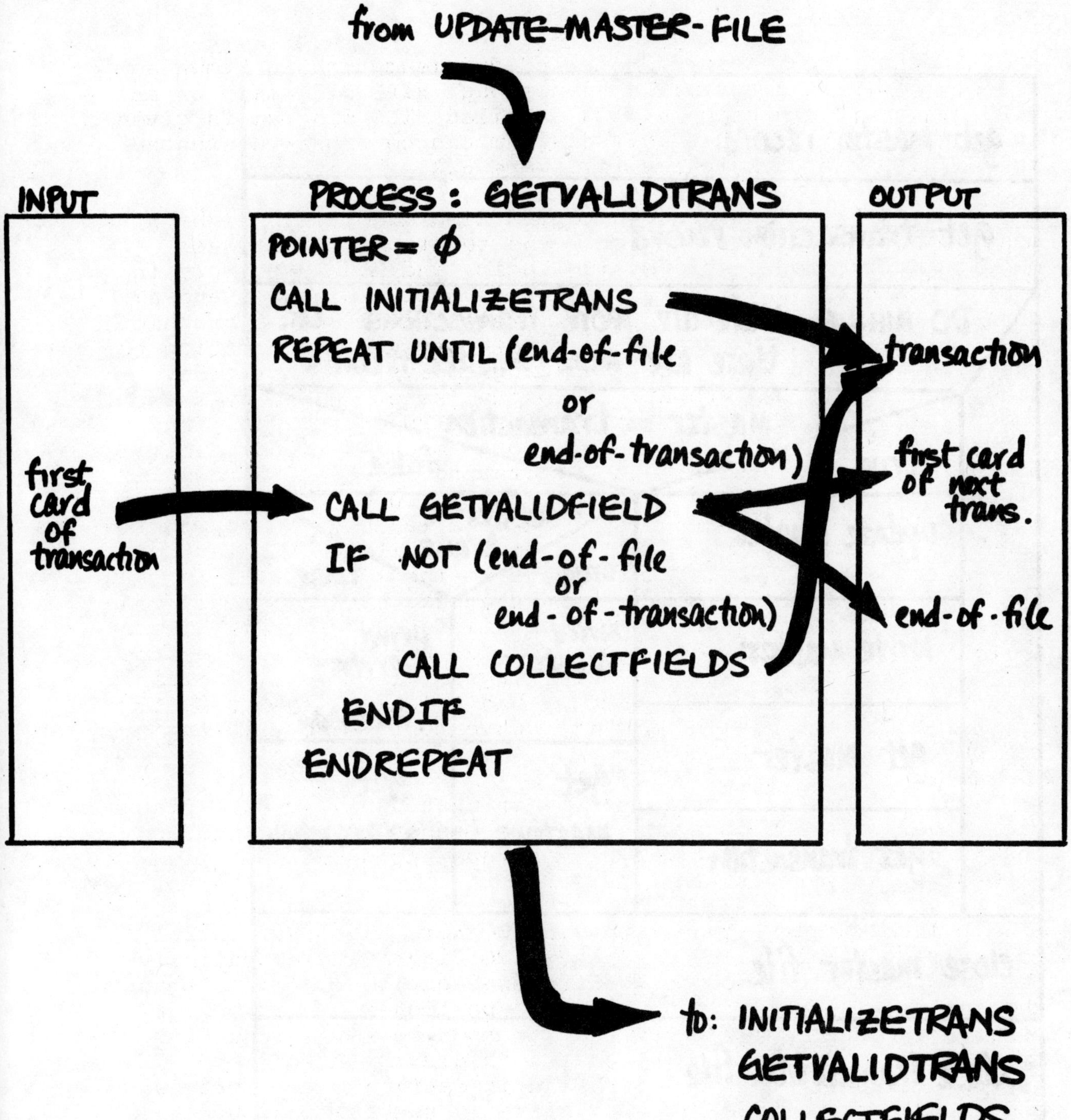

Figure 6.6: A typical Nassi-Schneiderman diagram.

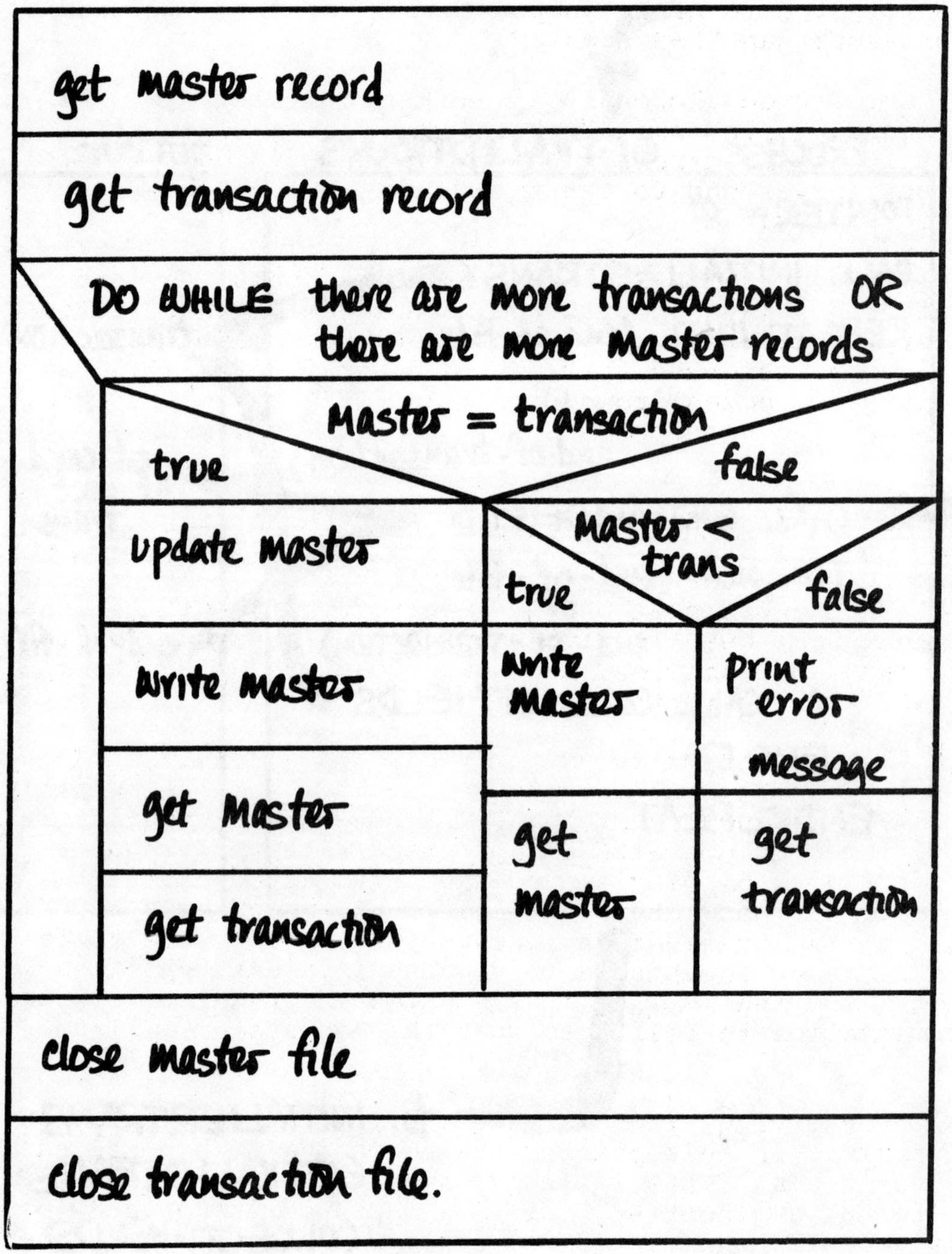

6.2.3 Nassi-Schneiderman diagrams

Figure 6.6 illustrates a third method of describing the detailed procedural logic within a module. This technique is known as a "Nassi-Schneiderman diagram," in honor of the two men who first published their ideas on the subject. On occasion, Figure 6.6 is referred to as a "Chapin chart," or a "structured flowchart," or simply an "N-S diagram."

Indeed, "structured flowchart" is an appropriate term. As we can see, Figure 6.6 is similar to a conventional flowchart -- except that it has no arrows. The three basic ideographs of the N-S diagrams correspond to the three basic constructs of structured programming.

The simplicity of the N-S diagram is quite appealing, and several organizations have adopted the technique for this reason alone. However, a number of organizations with whom I have spoken recently have observed that an N-S diagram is really just "pseudocode with some boxes around it." And if that is the case, why not just write the pseudocode?

6.3 Documentation Associated with Systems Analysis

There is a vast amount of other documentation associated with a typical EDP development project: narrative specifications, cost-benefit analyses, quantitative studies of processing volumes, file layouts, data dictionaries, documentation for the computer operations staff, and so forth.

While it is somewhat of an oversimplification, my opinion is that much, if not all, such documentation will remain basically unchanged by the introduction of the PPT techniques in your organization. The computer operations department will *still* require certain information to be provided to them in a "standard" fashion, so that they know what tapes to mount, which jobs to run, etc. The format of files and records will *still* have to be documented in a manner acceptable to various interested parties in the project. And the user community will *still* require various forms of documentation to tell them what the new system will do for them.

It *is* worth observing, though, that many of the documentation techniques described in this chapter are beginning to be used as systems analysis tools. That is, many organizations have discovered -- often by accident -- that *users* can understand data flow diagrams and HIPO charts and pseudocode. In some cases, the computerese jargon has to be eliminated (e.g., "pseudocode" sounds more acceptable if it is called "structured English"), but the content is quite intelligible to the average user.

6.4 Management Problems with the New Documentation Techniques

In the previous sections of this chapter, we alluded to the primary problem associated with the new documentation techniques -- the danger that they may suffer the same fate as detailed flowcharts. You should be prepared for this problem, particularly if you decide to adopt detailed HIPO diagrams, Nassi-Schneiderman diagrams, or even pseudocode in your organization.

Indeed, you should even be prepared for the fact that your programmers -- lazy devils that they may be -- may not keep the HIPO hierarchy charts (or structure charts) up-to-date. My personal experience has been that programmers *can* usually be browbeaten into redrawing the high-level structure charts whenever a change is made to the design (since the overall design changes much less frequently than the detailed logic within a module), but I have also heard bitter complaints from programmers who resented being forced to redraw a complicated diagram of the nature shown in Figure 6.3 just because one module interface has been changed, or one new module added to the system.

Some of the problem could be eliminated if we had more *automated* documentation packages. It should be practicable to develop packages to draw Nassi-Schneiderman diagrams (from structured code, of course!), and packages to draw high-level HIPO diagrams. Developing a package to draw detailed HIPO diagrams of the nature shown in Figure 6.5 would be much more difficult (unless one can find a way of drawing "fat" arrows on a plotter) -- and I doubt that we will see one commercially available in the near future.

The other major problems you should be prepared for when introducing the new documentation techniques are:

- "religious" interpretations of some of the documentation techniques
- the myth that using the documentation techniques is equivalent to the act of "design"

The problem of "religious" interpretations of the documentation techniques seems to be found primarily with HIPO: Some organizations have formulated extremely stringent standards concerning the manner in which HIPO diagrams will be drawn -- and at a certain point, one ends up drawing diagrams to satisfy the standards manual, rather than diagrams to illustrate a computer system.

It is the second problem area that concerns me more. I occasionally have asked programmers if they are using structured design, only to get the following answer: "Oh, yes, we're using structured design -- we're drawing lots of HIPO diagrams!"

Thousands of HIPO diagrams! We're really into structured design!" Implicit in this statement is the assumption that drawing a HIPO diagram is the same as *doing* a design.

You should be quite sure that your programmers understand the distinction between *documentation convention* and *design principles*. There are many programmers, for example, who would argue that the structure chart shown in Figure 6.3 is bad. You can imagine the following dialogue, which I have had with several programmers from time to time:

Manager: "What do you think of this structure chart in Figure 6.3?"

Charlie: "I don't like it.... It's bad."

Manager: "Why? What's wrong with it?"

Charlie: "Well ... one thing that I don't like is that the diagram shows that a level-2 module calls a level-6 module, four levels beneath it."

Manager: "What's wrong with that?"

Charlie: "Well, that's not the way they do it in HIPO."

Manager: "So what?"

Charlie: "Well, I just don't like it.... I think it would be a better design -- at least it would *look* better -- if some additional modules were introduced at levels 3, 4, and 5, so that we could always maintain the convention that a module calls only those modules that are one level beneath it."

The problem here is that Charlie has a certain feeling about the way the diagram should look; apparently, the form and symmetry of HIPO appeal to him. While I can't complain about that, it *does* bother me that Charlie's feeling about the preferred form of a *picture* would lead him to the conclusion that the *design* in Figure 6.3 is bad!

Chapter 6: References

1. *HIPO: A Design Aid and Documentation Technique*, IBM manual, Form GC20-1851-0.

2. Myers, Glenford J., *Reliable Software Through Composite Design*, Petrocelli/Charter, 1975. Myers presents a variation of structure charts -- sort of a compromise between the official version of HIPO, and the kind of structure chart shown in Figure 6.3.

3. Yourdon, Edward, and Larry Constantine, *Structured Design*, YOURDON inc., 1975. Chapters 3 and 4 of this book discuss structure charts. The appendix contains a detailed set of guidelines for drawing structure charts.

Chapter 7 HOW TO MANAGE CHIEF PROGRAMMER TEAMS

Chapters 7, 8, and 9 discuss some of the organizational concepts that have been introduced into the EDP community along with structured programming, structured design, and top-down implementation.

This chapter discusses the concept of the "chief programmer team organization," or "CPTO." It *could* have been a very lengthy chapter, but my experiences of the past two or three years suggest that there is not much point: Most organizations in the "real world" are *not* using the CPTO concept -- and have no intention of doing so in the foreseeable future. In most of the cases I have seen, I understand and agree with the decisions these organizations have made.

Consequently, this chapter will take on a somewhat less positive approach than the others in the book. As in the previous chapters, I will provide a brief overview of the CPTO concept. In addition, I will point out the reasons why your organization probably will not even attempt to implement the concept.

7.1 The Motivation Behind the CPTO Concept

Much of the motivation for the chief programmer team has been discussed in previous chapters. We can summarize it as follows:

- a growing awareness of the Peter Principle
- a realization of vast differences in programmer ability
- a realization of the communication problems inherent in large, classical, programming organizations.

The Peter Principle, you may recall, suggests that in most organizations, people are promoted until they reach their level of incompetence. There is an important corollary to the Peter Principle, too:

> After a certain period of time, all positions in a company are filled by people incompetent to perform them.

Thus, in the computer field, we find that good computer operators become junior programmers; good junior programmers become senior programmers; good senior programmers become systems analysts; good systems analysts become project leaders; and good project leaders are promoted into the upper echelons of DP management, where they may or may not be competent.

It is precisely this phenomenon that is one of the major motivations for the CPTO concept. Programmers have an understandable desire to earn more money and gain more stature in their organization -- and this can usually be done only by moving into management. And, of course, having reached the level of project leader, most people consider it beneath their dignity to write code -- and even if they would *like* to indulge in a little coding, they don't have time.

The chief programmer team concept is seen as a solution to this dilemma. The title "chief programmer" is considered analogous to the title "chief scientist" or "chief engineer" in other disciplines -- a master of his or her craft, with great skill and many years of experience. If such an environment could be created, the programmer would have the feeling that there was some honor in being recognized as a master craftsman -- and he would have some tangible incentive if his organization provided the kind of salary and status that it provided to high-level managers.

What kind of salary? How about $50,000 per annum? In some cases, it might be more appropriate to pay $75,000 or even $100,000 a year. Get the picture? We're talking about *big* money -- and you can imagine that such salaries would have quite an impact on the programmers' acceptance of the CPTO concept.

Having gone this far, we should mention the second major motivation behind the CPTO concept: the recognition that there is an order-of-magnitude difference in the abilities of programmers. We pointed out in Chapter 2 that Sackman's experiment suggests that the range in talent among *experienced, competent* programmers could be as much as a factor of 25!

If that's the case, a very simple strategy suggests itself: Why not fire the vast majority of mediocre programmers and accomplish all of our work with a few hand-picked super-programmers? When we consider the numbers of secretaries, clerks, managers, and other support personnel that could also be eliminated by this wholesale removal of the "Mongolian hordes," it seems quite a bargain to pay our chief programmer the mere pittance of $100,000 per year.

That may be a rational argument, but there are three problems: (a) There are *very* few such talented superprogrammers in existence; (b) those who exist are very choosy about where they work, and will generally shun the medium-sized commercial organizations; and (c) most organizations won't pay a salary of $100,000 per year to a programmer even if it *is* rational.

Why? Why does an organization refuse to pay $100,000 to a programmer who can turn out the same amount of work as 25 programmers whose salaries are $16,000 each? The answer is that top management simply cannot understand the concept -- and the *reason* they can't understand the concept is that their company is not in the computer business. In general, the American Widget Company is in the business of making widgets; their computer department is a necessary evil that exists only to print invoices, paychecks, and other such documents. Top management might be able to understand the concept of paying $100,000 a year to their chief widget designer, but the notion of paying such an outrageous salary to someone in their (ugh!) data processing department is unthinkable.

As a result, top management is also unimpressed with the third motivation of the CPTO approach: the recognition that communication problems between programmers become unmanageable on large projects. Indeed, many organizations do not recognize this as a problem, since their projects involve only three or four programmers.

The problem becomes noticeable with projects involving 20 or 30 programmers -- and becomes painfully obvious in projects involving 100 or 200 programmers. The meetings, and the memos, and interface documents, and standards manuals all attempt to maintain some semblance of communication -- but it is exceedingly difficult.

One reason for the difficulty is the individual programmer's habit of taking initiative whenever he has the opportunity. In a typical project, each programmer is given a module to design, code, and test; however, the chances are that the interface between his module and the rest of the system has not been defined very precisely. As a result, each programmer takes the initiative to define his interfaces a bit more precisely -- or, in some cases, makes some "teensy-weensy" changes to the defined interfaces. And with 20 or 30 programmers making independent design decisions in this fashion, things can get pretty chaotic!

With a chief programmer team, one usually finds the communication problems greatly reduced. First, the chief programmer's superhuman talents mean that far fewer people are required on the project -- and that alone reduces the communication problems significantly. Secondly, the chief programmer makes all of the critical design decisions; she (or he) tells the other programmers on the project what to do, and what the interfaces to their modules will be; and she (or he) enforces these interfaces with an iron hand.

With an approach like this, we find that one person -- the chief programmer -- has the "big picture" at all times; in contrast, many "conventional" projects are characterized by the fact that *nobody* really understands the whole system. In addition, the chief programmer approach means that -- in theory, at least -- the subordinate members of the team do not have to talk to each other to find out what is happening. Thus, instead of [N . (N-1)] ÷ 2 lines of communication between the N programmers in the project, we find that there are only (N-1) lines of communication.

7.2 The History of the CPTO Concept

Some organizations seem to feel that they have been using the chief programmer team concept for years. Indeed, I often visit organizations whose managers tell me, "Oh, yes, we've been doing this for quite some time.... Charlie, here, is our resident superprogrammer." In most cases, Charlie turns out to be a slightly-better-than-average programmer, but no superstar. And the "team" aspect of the CPTO approach (which we'll discuss later in this chapter) is usually completely missing.

On the other hand, many of the computer manufacturing organizations -- and some software consulting firms -- have *truly* used the chief programmer team concept for a decade or two. The smaller computer firms, for example, have known for quite some time that they could only compete with IBM, Honeywell, and Univac if they could develop their operating systems and compilers with small teams of two or three geniuses.

Two or three people to develop an operating system ... that would have been an interesting suggestion to make to IBM during their development of OS/360 in the mid-1960's! IBM frequently has become involved in massive development projects with hundreds (if not thousands) of programmers -- and has seen firsthand some of the problems discussed in previous chapters. Thus, it is not surprising (for those of us who have a somewhat positive attitude toward IBM) that IBM took the lead in formalizing and articulating some of the concepts that other computer vendors had been using unofficially for years.

IBM's first experiments with the CPTO approach occurred on the NASA Manned Spacecraft System in the mid-1960's. The next experiment -- a more formal one, and a more widely discussed one -- was the famous New York Times system. Since then, IBM and various other organizations have implemented a substantial number of CPTO projects. The stories of the early superprogrammer projects are fascinating, but not really germane to this book; if you are seriously interested in the CPTO approach, I recommend that you read some of the papers and books listed at the end of this chapter.

7.3 The Nature of the Chief Programmer Team

So far, we have referred in a rather loose fashion to superprogrammer, chief programmer, and chief programmer *team*. Who are these people? What do they do?

Following the terminology of Fred Brooks,* we can identify approximately ten *different* types of people on a chief programmer team:

- the chief programmer
- the copilot
- the administrator
- the editor
- the secretary
- the librarian
- the toolsmith
- the tester
- the language lawyer
- the programmer

We will discuss each of these team members briefly.

7.3.1 The chief programmer

The chief programmer is also referred to as the "surgeon" by Fred Brooks. To quote Brooks, the chief programmer "...needs great talent, ten years of experience, and considerable systems and application knowledge, whether in applied mathematics, business data processing or whatever."

From the comments that we have already made, we assume that the chief programmer is an excellent designer; is familiar with the features of operating systems, data base packages, structured programming, and structured design concepts; and is capable of coding ten to twenty times faster than the other programmers in the organization. To put this into perspective, IBM's Joel Aron reported, "Of the 2,000 programmers on the NASA project, only a handful would qualify as chief programmers."** Other organizations have suggested that only one out of 200 programmers is qualified to be a chief programmer; indeed, one authority in the field has suggested that there are only 12 chief programmers in the entire world!

In addition to being a superbly gifted technician, it is assumed that the chief programmer personally defines the functional specifications for the system; this means that he

---

*Fred Brooks, *The Mythical Man-Month*, Addison-Wesley, 1975.

**Joel Aron, "The Superprogrammer Project," *Software Engineering Techniques and Concepts*, J.M. Buxton, P. Naur, and B. Randell (Editors), Petrocelli/Charter, 1976.

must be conversant with the user's application, and be able to express it in a form intelligible to the user. Of course, many managers argue that a superprogrammer is unlikely to be able to do this well -- which is one of the reasons Brooks and IBM argue that there are so few people qualified for the job. To put it another way, merely being a superprogrammer is not enough to be considered a *chief* programmer.

Not only does the chief programmer define the functional specifications, he personally *designs* the entire system. Indeed, it is assumed that he writes all of the critical code in the system (e.g., the top-level modules, and some of the more complex modules in other parts of the system). He may even write *all* of the code.

What else could we possibly ask the chief programmer to do? Well, it turns out that the chief programmer is responsible for writing *all* of the documentation for the system -- user manuals, structure charts, Nassi-Schneiderman diagrams, narrative descriptions, and anything else that may be required. Clearly, this requires that the chief programmer have some command of the English language -- a capability one finds sorely lacking in many programmers!

Anything else? Just one more thing: The chief programmer is responsible for supervising the other members of the team. Thus, the chief programmer must have management capabilities -- although that aspect of his job is not assumed to occupy much of his time.

Our chief programmer, then, is a truly marvelous person: a combination of manager, superprogrammer, superdesigner, technical writer, and analyst. You can appreciate why there are arguments that such people -- if there *are* any such people -- deserve a salary of $100,000 per year!

7.3.2 The copilot

The term "copilot" is used in Brooks' discussion of chief programmer teams; it is common in other IBM literature to see the phrase "backup programmer."

The copilot is generally an apprentice chief programmer, although he may be (or may have been) a *real* chief programmer on other projects. His purpose is to serve as the chief programmer's "alter ego": He shares in the design work, and knows the code intimately. In addition, the copilot researches alternative design strategies and serves as a sounding board for some of the chief programmer's crazier ideas.

One of the other important functions of the copilot is *insurance:* If the chief programmer should be forced to leave the project, the copilot will probably be able to take over. In a less dramatic sense, we could imagine the chief programmer phasing out of a project during the final stages, leaving the copilot behind to finish off the last few detailed modules (note that with a top-down approach, the copilot would *not* be left with the unpleasant job of "system testing" at the end of the project).

On the negative side, we make the following observation: If it is hard to find *one* chief programmer for a project, it will be all that more difficult to find *two* such highly talented people for a single project.

7.3.3 The administrator

The administrator is the member of the team responsible for worrying about money, budgets, allocation of machine time, and other paperwork jobs. This function is most important in projects where there are substantial legal, contractual, or financial dealings.

Interestingly, most organizations would refer to such a person as the "project manager" -- and yet, in the CPTO approach, this person is *subordinate* to the chief programmer. Such an approach *has* been used in other fields, but it is considered rather novel -- indeed, radical! -- in most EDP organizations. The usual reaction is, "What!? You're suggesting that the project manager should report to some programmer who makes all the decisions? You've gotta be kidding!"

7.3.4 The editor

As we have already mentioned, the chief programmer is responsible for generating all documentation for a project. We assume that the chief programmer actually *writes* the documentation, thus ensuring the greatest possible technical accuracy and clarity.

However, we can imagine an editor who makes grammatical corrections to the chief programmer's rough drafts; provides references and bibliographies, where appropriate; and, perhaps most important, oversees the mechanical aspects of producing the documentation.

7.3.5 The secretary

A formal chief programmer team is actually assumed to have *two* secretaries -- one for the administrator, and one for the editor. The secretaries carry out the normal clerical duties of typing, filing, and so forth.

7.3.6 The program librarian

The program librarian is responsible for maintaining all of the technical records (source programs, listings, etc.) associated with the new project, and is quite distinct from the secretary mentioned above.

There is a great deal of discussion concerning the program librarian -- and, interestingly, this is *one* aspect of the chief programmer team that *has* been widely adopted. Indeed, the program librarian seems such a useful concept that Chapter 8 is devoted to it.

7.3.7 The toolsmith

The toolsmith is responsible for providing any specialized program development tools required by the chief programmer. These might include specialized utility programs (e.g., tape-to-printer of a variety not provided by the vendor); catalogued procedures and JCL; macro libraries (e.g., structured programming macros for assembly language); and any text-editing, file-editing, or debugging tools.

In many conventional projects, such tools may exist as part of a general-purpose library; on the other hand, the chief programmer may feel that he needs some *special* utilities. Also, we note that the tool-building aspect of the project may be only a part-time job; thus, the toolsmith might be able to serve more than one chief programmer team.

7.3.8 The tester

Basically, the tester is a person who develops test data that can be used for module testing and system testing. The tester may develop some of his test data from the functional specifications, without regard to the code; other test data may be developed *after* the tester has seen the code. In addition, the tester may develop test harnesses, dumps, traces, and other special testing/debugging packages.

Some CPTO projects assign the tester function to the copilot; others ask the user to develop test data. In a large project, though, generation of test data and test utilities can be a full-time job -- and it may require certain talents (and a certain kind of psychology) that can only be found in a full-time tester.

7.3.9 The language lawyer

The language lawyer is considered to be the expert in various detailed parts of the programming environment -- the operating system, the data base management package, the compiler, the JCL for the system, and so forth.

The language lawyer exists to answer the following sort of questions: "What really happens -- at the assembly language level -- when I execute a MOVE CORRESPONDING statement in COBOL?" or, "Does the current version of the operating system *really* implement the XYZ system call correctly?" or, "What's the fastest way of zeroing a table in assembly language on the Widget computer?"

These are all things that the chief programmer might be expected to know himself -- particularly "static" pieces of information like the fastest way of zeroing a table on a particular computer. Much of the information, though, is dynamic: It changes with each new release of the vendor's compiler or operating system. And it is information that is usually buried in the small print in the appendix of some manual -- if it exits at all.

Thus, while the chief programmer is probably smart enough to be able to find the answers to questions of the sort posed above, he prefers to draw upon the knowledge of the language lawyer.

7.3.10 The programmer

On small-to-medium size projects, the programmer may not exist -- all of the coding may be done by the chief programmer. On medium-to-large size projects, the programmer writes code that has been specified and possibly designed by the chief programmer.

7.4 Management Problems with the Chief Programmer Team

I have suggested throughout this chapter that there are problems with the chief programmer team. The problems can be summarized as follows:

1. Chief programmers are very *hard* to find. Many organizations make the mistake of assuming that their most-senior programmers are "chief programmers" -- beware! Other organizations fall into the trap of believing the reputation of some of their programmers: Charlie, for example, has the reputation of being a superprogrammer -- perhaps only because he knows more obscure instructions in the programming language than the other programmers. And many organizations find that they have some programmers who can code quickly -- but who cannot document and who cannot carry on a reasonable conversation with the user, and who cannot supervise other people; such "supercoders" are *not* chief programmers.

2. It is difficult to convince organizations to compensate the chief programmer properly. Some organizations claim that they have "dual career paths," but that usually turns out to be mostly hot air.

3. Even with appropriate pay and fringe benefits, it is difficult to convince a chief programmer to work for a typical company. Why should he waste his time writing another payroll system on IBM System/3 in RPG-II, when he could be working for a more glamorous firm with an on-line, real-time, multi-processor 370/168 system?

4. It is difficult to organize a chief programmer team to fit into the classical organization structure of most companies. Theoretically, the chief programmer is in charge of the chief programmer team. But where does that leave the project manager in today's organization -- that's *you,* dear reader! Are you willing to be replaced by a 22-year-old superprogrammer?

5. It is difficult to reconcile the chief programmer team concept with the classical view of the systems analyst. Theoretically, the systems analyst (if one exists at all) would be subordinate to the chief programmer -- and that is just the *opposite* of the political structure in most organizations. Indeed, the purist CPTO approach suggests that we need no systems analysts at all, since the chief programmer can carry out that function. So what do we do with the systems analysts currently employed in our company? Shoot them?

6. Finally, it is difficult to introduce the chief programmer team concept into an organization that currently employs large hordes of mediocre programmers. What does one do with the Mongolian hordes? Shoot them? Fire them? Let them die of old age?

These are not easy questions to answer --- and it is interesting that the people who must provide the answers are often those whose empires, whose political stature, and whose very jobs are threatened by the CPTO approach.

As a result, the majority of EDP organizations that I have visited have abandoned the CPTO concept. A few organizations have given their old senior (and possibly mediocre) programmers the new title of "Chief Programmer," and deluded themselves into thinking that they have adopted the CPTO concept.

And several organizations have adopted those aspects of the CPTO approach that *can* fit into their current method of doing business. In particular, we find that the program librarian concept is being widely adopted; we will discuss this further in Chapter 8. And we find that the structured walkthrough concept -- or "egoless programming" concept -- is being widely adopted; we will discuss this in Chapter 9.

So, if *you* meet someone from an organization that says it is practicing the chief programmer team approach, find out if their chief programmer can really code with both hands, walk on water, leap over tall buildings in a single bound -- and chew gum at the same time. Chances are he can't. Chances are the organization has introduced walkthroughs, and program librarians -- and labelled the result a "chief programmer team."

Chapter 7: References

1. Aron, Joel, "The Superprogrammer Project," *Software Engineering Techniques and Concepts*, J.M. Buxton, P. Naur, and B. Randell (Editors), Petrocelli/Charter, 1976.

2. Baker, F.T., "Chief Programmer Team Management of Production Programming," *IBM Systems Journal*, January 1972.

3. Brooks, Fred, *The Mythical Man-Month*, Addison-Wesley, 1975.

4. Mills, Harlan, and F.T. Baker, "Chief Programmer Teams," *Datamation*, December 1973.

Chapter 8 HOW TO MANAGE PROGRAM LIBRARIANS

As we pointed out in the previous chapter, most EDP organizations have *not* adopted the concept of a team of specialists built around a superprogrammer. However, one aspect of the chief programmer team concept *has* begun to gain wide acceptance: the *program librarian*.

This chapter, written on the assumption that you may wish to consider the use of program librarians independently of the CPTO concept, begins with an overview of the librarian concept, and includes a discussion of the qualifications for librarians, the duties of the librarian, and the concept of a Development Support Library. We will conclude with a discussion of the problems you are likely to encounter with the librarian concept in your organization.

8.1 The Objectives of the Librarian Concept

The concept of a formal librarian is usually associated with IBM's early experiments with the chief programmer team in the mid-1960's. From the very beginning, there have been two major objectives of the librarian:

- to make programmers more productive by eliminating the clerical part of their work
- to organize and control all of the technical information generated by the programming team, thus eliminating much of the chaos presently found in EDP development projects.

You may recall from Chapter 2 that there are some statistics to support that first objective: Weinwurm's study indicates that the average programmer spends only 27% of his day actually programming! Your programmers may spend more of their time programming -- but it should be obvious to you as manager that a substantial part of your programmers' activities are clerical in nature.

The significance of this point has been confirmed in a number of recent PPT projects. IBM, for example, reports the following: Two programmers supported by a librarian are generally as productive as three programmers working alone. Some of my clients have gone even further: They report that one programmer supported by a librarian is equivalent to two programmers without clerical support.

The other motivation for the librarian concept is more difficult to quantify. Nevertheless, it is very clear that most EDP development projects need *much* more clerical organization than they currently have. At the moment, every programmer tends to keep his own private file of source programs, his own listings, his own special patches to the system, and so forth.

To appreciate the significance of this problem, put yourself in the position of the development programmer. Imagine that you have been told that the only reason a new system doesn't work is because of a bug in *your* module. Since you can't get any machine time during the day, you decide to come into work in the middle of the night to fix the bug in your module. In the midst of your debugging -- about 3 o'clock in the morning -- you discover that the bug is *not* in your module, but instead in Fred's module.

Being a civilized person, you decide not to call Fred and wake him from a peaceful sleep. Instead, you walk into Fred's office to retrieve a copy of his program listing -- to see if you can discover the nature of the problem. Unfortunately, you find, in Fred's office, not just *one* program listing, but some ten or twenty -- all of which are marked "new," "current," and "experimental." Which version of Fred's module is supposed to be the "official" version? Have you been using the right version in your debugging activities. Or have you wasted an entire night debugging with an obsolete (or experimental) version of Fred's module?

There is another scenario that is sometimes more accurate: It turns out that Fred is paranoid, and has locked all of his listings in his desk. And it turns out that Fred has just left for a three-week fishing trip in the wilds of Lower Slobovia where he can't be reached by phone....

With this kind of scenario -- which is all too common in the data processing industry -- you can see why there has been such a strong argument in favor of the librarian concept. There is another way of looking at it: What we are saying is that the development programming groups should have the same degree of control over source programs, listings, and object modules as the maintenance department has had for years. Maintenance groups could not survive if they permitted the chaos currently found in most development groups -- and development groups are beginning to find that they can't survive either.

8.2 Qualifications for Librarians

Having introduced the general notion of a librarian, we are now in a position to discuss the kind of person best suited to be librarian. I must emphasize that there are a number of very different opinions in this area -- *all* of which are right!

The librarian can be whatever you want him/her* to be -- and you should select the kind of person you want depending on the kind of duties you want the librarian to perform.

While there may be differing points of view concerning the nature of the librarian, there seems to be three *common* views:

- *Clerical.* Someone who is competent at typing, keypunching, filing, organizing, and acting as a "gopher" -- go for this, go for that....

- *Programming.* Someone who can interact with a time-sharing system, someone who can talk to operators, someone who understands a little of what programmers are talking about.

- *Managerial.* Someone who has sufficient personal "presence" and strength of personality to *effectively* control access to source programs, listings, etc. Someone who is capable of reporting on the status of a project to the manager.

Probably the most common type of librarian is the clerical person. A great deal of the usefulness of the librarian is associated with the simple clerical burden that programmers currently have to bear. A HIPO diagram has to be redrawn; who's going to do it? A program has to be taken downstairs to the computer room to be compiled; who will take it? A legible, but handwritten, page of coding has to be transcribed onto coding sheets before the keypunch department will accept it; who will be responsible? All of these tasks require nothing more than an intelligent, well-organized clerk.

Some organizations find that a secretary who has already worked in a programming department makes an excellent librarian -- if the librarian's job is defined strictly as a clerical function. Other companies have recruited people from the keypunch department, or from other areas of the organization that are involved in data processing in a peripheral fashion.

Other organizations seem to stress the notion of a librarian as "junior apprentice programmer." Such a librarian is *not* a programmer -- but, on the other hand, he/she does not find the computer programming environment totally alien. Thus, a librarian might be any one of the following: a student in a

---

*Discussions about librarians have an unfortunate tendency to take on sexist overtones. To avoid such inferences, I will use the phrase "he/she" and "him/her" wherever appropriate.

computer science curriculum from a local university (especially a co-op student who works on-the-job for six months at a time); a junior computer operator (senior computer operators may feel that becoming a librarian constitutes a loss of status); an RJE terminal operator; a senior, intelligent, keypunch operator (the type that has been correcting the programmer's COBOL coding errors for years); or one of the various types of programmers who cannot stand the intellectual, physical, and psychological rigors of being a "real" programmer.

Finally, some organizations have suggested that the librarian may be a person with management talents. This is by no means as crazy as it may sound: If the librarian is responsible for controlling access to the vital documents (programs, listings, etc.) associated with a project, it would be helpful for him/her to have the strength, intelligence, and force of personality that one might expect of a future manager. In addition to that, the librarian is in the rather unique position of knowing the current *status* of the development project (which modules have been compiled and which have not, which modules have been tested and which have not, etc.), which is precisely the kind of information the project manager wants to know. Thus, a few organizations regard their librarians as the project manager of the future.

The conclusion: *You* have to decide whether your librarian should be a simple clerk, an apprentice programmer, or a fledgling project manager. One other suggestion: The word "librarian" may not be the most diplomatic job title in some cases. You might decide that it would be more appropriate -- diplomatically and politically -- to call such a person a "junior computer systems officer, grade 1," or a "systems maintenance technician," or a "programmer's assistant," or a "programming technician," or some other title.

8.3 Duties of the Librarian

The librarian's duties obviously depend to a large extent on the kind of person you select -- and on your view of the librarian as a "clerk," a "junior programmer," or a "junior manager."

Most organizations, though, define the librarian's duties as some combinations of those described below:

1. *Accept "raw" source programs.* The librarian is usually expected to accept code written by the programmer on a coding sheet, or written longhand on ordinary paper. One or two experiments have even been tried with the programmer dictating his code into a tape recorder!

2. *Prepare a machine-readable source program.* This may require the librarian to actually keypunch the program, or to type the program into a time-sharing terminal. More commonly, though, the librarian is required to supervise someone else's keypunching -- i.e., the librarian has to take the coding sheets to the keypunch department, check periodically to see if the keypunching has been done, and finally bring the keypunched program back.

3. *Arrange for compilations/assemblies.* This task may require the librarian to put some standard control cards (JCL) on the front of the program; the librarian may not understand the details of those control cards, but may simply be aware that that is part of the magic process known as "compile." The librarian may also be required to take the source program to the computer room to be compiled; or he/she may be required to direct the compilation from a time-sharing terminal or RJE terminal. Presumably, the librarian would also be required to bring a copy of the compiler output back to the programmer. If the librarian's job is defined as that of a "junior apprentice programmer," then he/she may be required to correct trivial keypunch errors and syntax errors (and carry out appropriate recompilations of the program) before bringing it back to the programmer.

4. *File copies of appropriate documents in a library.* As we mentioned earlier, one of the more important functions of the librarian is to ensure controlled access to source programs, listings, etc. This usually implies that the critical documents are filed in a library -- the nature of which is discussed in the following section.

5. *Carry out editing, recompiling, and other maintenance activities.* In most cases, the programmer will want to correct bugs, make changes, and add new code to the initial version of his program. This is usually accomplished by allowing the programmer to submit a marked-up program listing to the librarian -- who then repeats many of the steps described above. Note, by the way, that the marked-up listing also should be filed in the library.

6. *Carry out executions and test runs of programs.* The librarian may use standard control cards or JCL for this function; or the programmer may provide special instructions. In any case, the librarian's function remains the same: to take over the clerical burden of such tasks, and to maintain control over the associated documents. One of the most common -- and most important -- examples of this task is something we might call "system building": From time to time, the librarian will gather together all of the official versions of individual modules and "build" (or "link" or "link edit") a new official version of the entire system.

8.4 The Development Support Library

In most cases, each project and each company develop slightly different standards and procedures for the librarian -- and for the library maintained by the librarian. However, we normally find the following *types* of information maintained by the librarian:

1. *Handwritten documents.* This part of the library would presumably be maintained in ordinary file cabinets, and would contain such things as original source programs (on coding sheets), marked-up program listings, original handwritten test data, and programmers' instructions for test runs.

2. *Machine-readable documents.* This part of the library would be maintained on the computer system itself, perhaps with the assistance of such "packages" as PANVALET, LIBRARIAN, etc. Such a library would primarily consist of source programs, object modules, load modules, test files, etc. Note that "prior" versions of such files would be maintained in addition to the current version.

3. *Program listings.* It is possible, of course, to maintain the program listings on a computer file (e.g., tape or disk) along with the source programs and object modules; however, the volume of program listings usually makes this prohibitive. Thus, the library would include, as one of its major elements, an official copy of the program listing of all of the modules of the system, plus appropriate back-up listings.

4. *Operating instructions.* This part of the library consists of run books and standard JCL for editing, compiling, executing, and testing programs. On IBM machines, this would probably consist of "catalogued procedures"; on other systems, it might consist of specially punched control cards.

5. *Library maintenance information.* This part of the library is an index: It indicates where everything is stored, how to access it, what procedures are used to update information, etc. The primary purpose of this set of information is to provide insurance in case the librarian is absent from the project -- or suddenly disappears from the project.

8.5. Management Problems with the Librarian Concept

As with the other PPT techniques, you should be prepared for problems when introducing the librarian concept into your organization. The problems emanate from three different areas of the organization: from higher echelons of management, from the programmers, and from the librarians themselves.

8.5.1 Problems with management

One of the problems you probably will find is a classical one when introducing a new *type* of job into the organization: The personnel department will tell you that there is no job description for "librarians." What civil service grade should he/she get? How much should he/she be paid? Unfortunately, there is no immediate, simple answer to these questions. It depends on precisely how the job is defined, and whether one selects a clerk, a junior trainee programmer, or a junior manager for the job. And, it can take six months to a year to provide the appropriate data to the personnel department. If you are working for a large, conservative organization, be prepared for some delays.

A more immediate problem faced by some organizations is the lack of money in the budget. As many EDP managers have told me, they are allowed to hire a certain number of "bodies" each year; it doesn't matter to the higher echelons of management whether those bodies are librarians or Ph.D. computer scientists. In other companies, things are even more simple: A hiring freeze may prevent the manager from hiring programmers *or* librarians.

A different kind of problem occurs in organizations in which the top-level DP management came from the programming ranks. You should be prepared for the following kind of reaction from your boss: "What's the matter with today's young whippersnappers? Why, when *I* was a programmer, we used to keypunch our own programs, and operate the computers ourselves! Today's programmers are too lazy to do their own work!"

Some of the problems in this area are understandable, even if they are frustrating. You can appreciate that the personnel department insists on formal job descriptions before it allows you to hire a librarian. You can appreciate that an economic slump has led to a general hiring freeze throughout the company. The only thing one could complain about is the reaction from higher echelons of management that programmers don't "deserve" librarians, that they should do their own "dirty work."

If you get this kind of reaction from your management, try to point out to them that your programmers are too highly paid to waste their time doing a job that *could* be done by a clerk with no more than an elementary school education. If your management demurs, they may be telling you that *they* view your programmers as nothing more than highly paid (if not *overpaid*) clerks -- and they don't understand why clerks should require subordinate clerks to help them do their job. An attitude like that may be fashionable in certain circles and is compatible with the belief that "someday we won't need programmers -- the users will simply talk to the computers, and the computers will program themselves." But it seems contrary to the notion that programming is a *profession*. Indeed, such an attitude from your management might be a signal that the time has come to begin circulating your resume to other, hopefully more progressive, organizations!

8.5.2 Problems with the programmers

It might not have occurred to you that the *programmers* would object to the introduction of librarians -- but occasionally they do. Sometimes the programmers are just being ornery, but they occasionally have some valid objections.

For example, some programmers complain that the librarian will simply be one more middleman between them and the machine. From this point of view, life was wonderful in the "good old days" when the programmer keypunched his own program, and operated his own programs in the computer room. Things started going downhill when computer operators were introduced; it got worse when the programmer was told to submit all of his keypunching to a separate department (which tended to lose his keypunching, or confuse his "oh's" and "zeroes"); and *now*, the programmer complains, you want to introduce a librarian!

Obviously, the librarian is not supposed to decrease the programmer's efficiency -- indeed, quite the opposite! On the other hand, the programmer's complaint in this area is a good warning: It tells us that we may well be defeating our cause if we set up a "pool" of librarians for the entire EDP organization. A "librarian department" may cause the same problems as the "keypunch department" -- simply because it is a separate political organization, with its own loyalties. There is another way to illustrate this situation: As a manager, would you rather have your memos and letters typed by your own secretary (whose habits and idiosyncrasies you have come to know) or by an anonymous member of the 100-person typing pool in your company? ... Your programmers feel the same way!

There is another common problem in some organizations: The programmers have access to time-sharing terminals and computerized "librarian" software packages -- and they don't see the need for a *human* librarian. This may be a valid point -- *if* there are sufficient terminals for the programmers, and *if* the programmers can type more than two or three characters a minute, and *if* the time-sharing system contains sufficient software to organize the various source programs and object modules in a controllable fashion.

You should also be prepared for the programmer who asks, "Gee, if I give all this work to the librarian, what's left for me to do?" This is often an indication that the programmer has a poor view of himself: If he thinks that he is *supposed* to be doing work that is primarily clerical, and if he can't think of anything better to do, something is terribly wrong....

Finally, be prepared for the programmer who thinks, "If I give all this work to the librarian, I won't have any excuse to get up from my desk and wander around -- I'll have to program eight hours a day!" To some extent, this complaint is valid: Serious design and coding can be a mentally fatiguing activity, and one needs to take an occasional break. This is rather difficult to do in some companies, and many programmers have found that one of the "safe" ways of relaxing for a few moments is to walk to the computer room to pick up some output from a test run, and then walk to the keypunch room to pick up the keypunching -- in other words, to deliberately take on some of the duties of the librarian.

Unfortunately, one sometimes gets the impression that the programmer is complaining that he really doesn't want to program eight hours a day, that programming is something unpleasant and difficult, something that he would like to do as little of as possible. If you sense *that* kind of reaction from your programmer, I would suggest either of two options: fire him/her, or make him/her a librarian!

8.5.3 Problems with the librarians

Finally, we should point out that you can have problems with the librarians themselves, whose complaints seem to fall into three categories:

- "I don't understand the job -- the terminology and the technology are alien to me."
- "I don't like working with programmers -- I would rather be working with human beings."
- "I'm bored with the job -- I want to be a programmer."

The first two objections are likely to come from librarians who have been recruited from the clerical ranks. One way of avoiding this problem -- as we implied earlier -- is to recruit your librarian from areas already associated with the EDP department. Thus, you should find that a person currently working as a secretary in the programming department can become a librarian without feeling such an acute sense of being stuck in an "alien" environment.

The third complaint -- that of boredom -- is most likely to come from librarians who have training, experience, and/or aptitude for programming. If you hire someone with a bachelor's degree in Computer Science, and put him/her to work as a librarian, you can expect to hear this complaint after a week or two. If you recruit someone from the computer operations department, you can expect such a complaint after a few months. Indeed, no matter *who* the librarian is, be prepared for this problem -- if he/she is bright and has absorbed some of the rudiments of programming.

Assuming that the librarian *is*, in fact, clever enough to become a programmer, you should let him/her make the jump. This implies, then, that your discussions with the personnel department (recall Section 8.5.1) should include a possible career path into programming.

Chapter 9 HOW TO MANAGE STRUCTURED WALKTHROUGHS

In the previous two chapters, we discussed two concepts that could have a major impact on the organization of programmers in your company. This chapter discusses another such "organizational" concept: structured walkthroughs. Walkthroughs are one of the more important activities of a programming team -- indeed, they can be an extremely important activity for *any* group of programmers, whether or not they work in teams.

What is a walkthrough? Why are walkthroughs usually associated with programming teams? Why do people use the term "structured walkthrough"? These questions are discussed in this chapter, following the format established in previous chapters: an overview of the technical concepts, and a discussion of the problems you are likely to face when implementing the techniques in your organization.

9.1 Egoless Teams

Before we can discuss the notion of "walk through a program," we need some background. The original idea of walkthroughs was motivated by Gerald Weinberg in his classic book, *The Psychology of Computer Programming.*

Weinberg's work introduced into the computer field such phrases as "egoless programming," "programming teams," democratic teams," "egoless teams," "adaptive teams," and even "programming families." One can draw analogies with efforts in other industries (e.g., such automobile companies as General Motors, Volvo, and Saab) to establish "teams" that are responsible for well-defined areas of production. One can also see large influences from such psychological fields as transactional analysis (e.g., the "I'm OK, you're OK" work of Eric Berne and others).

The purpose of teams in the programming field is primarily to change programming from "private art to public practice," as Harlan Mills puts it. Or, to use Weinberg's words, the intention is to change programs from "private works of art to corporate assets." That is, there is a growing recognition that many programmers have been working *alone* throughout their careers -- and have been more interested in the personal, intellectual pleasure of writing programs than they have been in seeing the programs work for the user.

A programming team -- if it is successful -- creates an environment in which everyone feels free to discuss and critique everyone else's programs. This discussion of other people's programs is usually formalized in a *walkthrough*, the major topic of this chapter.

There are many other aspects of egoless teams, as well -- many of which are sufficiently radical that the concept has not yet gained wide acceptance. For example, experience with egoless teams indicates that different people will emerge as the natural "leader" at different stages of the project: One team member may dominate during the design phase of the project, others may dominate during the coding, while still others may dominate during the debugging and testing.

Another aspect of the egoless team is that nobody is really "in charge" -- nobody is the boss, in the traditional sense. This generally makes outside management somewhat nervous ("Whose rear end are we going to kick if the project comes in behind schedule?"), although that problem sometimes can be circumvented by nominating one team member as the spokesperson for the group. The absence of a formal boss may also be difficult for some team members to handle -- a number of people are accustomed to, and would prefer, an authoritarian manager who tells them what to do.

Note also that the egoless team may not have any superprogrammers -- if it did, we would probably call it a chief programmer team. However, we observed in Chapter 7 that most companies don't have a superprogrammer anyway -- so maybe the egoless team is the best way to cope with the large numbers of average programmers a company employs.

Obviously, the mere act of putting three or four people into a project does not make them function as a *team*. Implicit in the concept of a team is the notion of working closely together, reading each other's code, sharing responsibilities, getting to know each other's idiosyncrasies (both on a technical and a personal level), and accepting a *group* responsibility for the product. If this attitude *can* be instilled, the effect is usually one of synergism: Five people working together on a team may produce twice as much as they would working individually.

We should make one other comparison between the chief programmer team and the egoless team. *If* you have a superprogrammer in your organization, the chances are that *he's* not egoless -- he's very good, and he's happy to tell everyone just how good he is. This may well destroy the democratic aspect of the team -- especially when it comes to walkthroughs. You may find that the chief programmer wants to review all of the code *by himself,* rather than making it a group activity -- and that sort of one-on-one confrontation between an individual programmer and the chief programmer is hardly likely to be egoless.

There are many who feel that egoless teams are the wave of the future. In organizations where such a concept has been successfully implemented, the results have been quite impressive -- and the programmers will generally tell you that they would never revert to their "old" way of doing things. On the other hand, many organizations have found that they simply cannot implement the concept: There are too many psychological problems, too many personality clashes, and too many political problems.

In summary, then, it seems that the concept of true programming "teams," or "families," will probably suffer the same fate as the chief programmer team concept. We will not discuss it further in this book, but I recommend that you read Weinberg's book if you find the idea interesting.

If egoless teams are a failure, why are we talking about them? And in any case, why are we talking about them in *this* chapter? The reason is very simple: About the only aspect of the team concept that is likely to be implemented in the typical organization is that of a walkthrough. Keep that in mind: Walkthroughs approximate team programming, and are one of the first steps toward establishing programming teams.

9.2 Types of Walkthroughs

Most discussions about walkthroughs concentrate on code: That is, people sometimes think that the only purpose of a walkthrough is to examine a program listing. In fact, we can imagine several different types of walkthroughs:

1. *Specification walkthroughs.* As the name implies, the primary purpose of this type of walkthrough is to look for problems, inaccuracies, ambiguities, and omissions in the *specification* of a system. Such a walkthrough would presumably involve the user, the systems analyst, and one or more programmers on the project.

2. *Design walkthroughs.* The purpose of this walkthrough is to look for flaws, weaknesses, errors, and omissions in the architecture of the design -- before code is written. This walkthrough might involve the user: It would certainly involve the systems analyst; it would involve the senior programmer (chief programmer) on the project, and probably all of the other programmers as well. The document used for this walkthrough would be the HIPO diagrams and structure charts discussed in Chapter 6.

3. *Code walkthroughs.* This is where the code is reviewed. A code review includes the programmer who wrote the code, the other programmers on the team, and, possibly, some programmers from outside the team.

4. *Test walkthroughs.* The purpose of this type of walkthrough is to ensure the adequacy of the test data for the system -- *not* to examine the output from the test run. Attendees at such a walkthrough would include the programmers on the project; the tester, if such a person exists (recall the discussion in Chapter 7); the systems analyst; and perhaps the user, if he can be enticed to join in the fun.

Specification walkthroughs, design walkthroughs, and test walkthroughs are not really a new idea -- except that they are usually called "reviews" in most organizations. The very phrase "design review" strikes terror into the hearts of most analysts and designers: It strongly implies a formal political ritual, in which users, analysts, and programmers spend an entire day yelling at each other and insulting each other's ancestry... while the "big bosses" from the user department and the programming department sit in the back of the room taking notes. Sometimes it is a political ritual of another kind: a dull meeting convened to rubber-stamp a design that nobody understands....

The point is that design reviews (and specification reviews) tend to be very formal, and somewhat political in nature. Of necessity, they tend to be global in their examination of a design. Because of the number of people involved, they can only be convened occasionally ... and since it is such a hassle getting the design review committee together, one feels obliged to make a formal presentation (complete with flip charts, foils, and 35mm slides) of the entire design.

By contrast, walkthroughs tend to be informal, and local in nature. The people who participate in the walkthrough may meet three times a week, or even three times a day. They discuss small parts of the design (or the specifications, or the code) quietly and informally -- and as a result, *much* more is usually accomplished!

We should make another point about the different types of walkthroughs listed above: It is important that they take place in the order listed! It is extremely unpleasant to discover in a *code* walkthrough that there was an error in the specifications; indeed, it is unpleasant to be told in a code walkthrough that the design is unacceptable to the rest of the team. By the time one begins designing, the team should have uncovered the major weaknesses in the specifications; by the time one begins coding, the team should have discovered the major problems in the design.

9.3 Objectives of a Walkthrough

Although they have been implied throughout this chapter, the objectives of a walkthrough should be spelled out. The major objective, of course, is to find errors: an omission, a contradiction, or a logical error of any kind. And walkthroughs are quite successful in this area: Weinberg reports that the number of errors in production systems has decreased by a factor of five in organizations that use walkthroughs diligently.

Another major objective of the walkthrough is to look for errors of "style." The walkthrough will usually point out major efficiency problems in the code, readability problems in the code (e.g., cryptic data names), modularity problems in the design, and unreasonable requirements in the specifications. It is in this area, of course, that arguments will arise: What is reasonable to one person will not necessarily seem reasonable to another!

There are other, somewhat less tangible objectives of a walkthrough. We notice, for example, that the mere threat of a walkthrough tends to improve the quality of the code, the design, the specifications, or the test data. Obviously, one does not want to look like a fool in front of one's peers. At the coding level, this sometimes translates into something more tangible: The other members of the team may be unwilling to walk through anything other than structured code developed in a top-down fashion.

It has also been observed that team reviews -- or walkthroughs -- serve as a consciousness-raising session for everyone. Not only do the junior people learn techniques from the senior people, but the senior people often get new ideas and new insights from the junior people. Weinberg also has a statistic in this area: He claims that one year working as part of a team (i.e., one that practices walkthroughs) is equivalent to two years of working alone.

Also, frequent walkthroughs minimize the chance of having to throw code away if someone is forced to leave the project. In conventional projects, we usually find that a half-finished program is worthless if the author of that program is forced to leave the project. A new programmer finds it impossible to figure out what the original programmer was doing -- so he throws the half-finished code away, and starts over again.

9.4 When Should a Walkthrough Be Conducted?

When should a walkthrough be conducted? Basically, the guideline is simple: A walkthrough should be conducted as frequently as possible, so that *small* pieces of code (or design, or specifications, or test data) are reviewed. At the same time, a walkthrough should be arranged only when the programmer is ready for one: One of the worst things you as a manager can do is legislate walkthroughs every Friday afternoon, or after every 100 lines of coding.

With specification walkthroughs and design walkthroughs, there is not much question about the documents that are required for the walkthrough, or the time at which it is reasonable to schedule a walkthrough. For code walkthroughs, things are different. One can imagine having a code walkthrough at any of the following stages:

- before the code is keypunched
- after the code is keypunched, but before it is compiled
- after the first compilation
- after the first clean compilation
- after the first test case has been executed successfully
- after the programmer thinks that *all* test cases have been executed successfully.

There are advantages and disadvantages of having walkthroughs at these various points in time. For example, it is relatively unpleasant conducting a walkthrough when the source document is a coding sheet, because (a) each reviewer probably has a nearly illegible photostat of a coding sheet whose instructions were written in pencil, and (b) each sheet of paper probably contains only 10 or 20 lines of information, which means that the reviewer is constantly turning the pages back and forth to see what the program is doing, and (c) the reviewer sorely misses symbol tables, cross-reference listings, and other helpful aids normally produced by the compiler or assembler.

On the other hand, there are often tremendous delays associated with the keypunching and compiling of a program. If this is the case, the team may wish to ensure that the code is correct before wasting a day (or as much as a week) waiting for it to be keypunched. It is for this same reason that some organizations conduct their walkthroughs after the code has been keypunched, but before it has been compiled -- the source document is usually a simple "80-80" listing produced by an EAM machine.

It is *much* more common, though, to conduct a walkthrough *after* the program has been compiled. At that point, the reviewers are working with a more legible document, with more information on each page -- and with the symbol tables, cross-reference listings, and other helpful information provided as a matter of course by the compiler. Some people argue that the walkthrough should not take place until the programmer has produced a clean compilation -- i.e., one without syntax errors. In most cases, this makes sense *if* your organization has reasonably good turnaround time for compilations. Obviously, you must strike a balance here: On the one hand, you don't want to waste the time of an entire team looking for syntax errors that can be found easily by a compiler. On the other hand, you don't want the author of the program to spend several days submitting his program for compilations over and over again in an attempt to get rid of difficult syntax errors.

It is usually considered a bad idea to delay the walkthrough until the programmer has begun testing his program -- and definitely a bad idea to wait until the programmer *thinks* he has finished *all* of his testing. First of all, a great deal of time has probably been wasted in this kind of approach: The programmer generally spends a great deal of time beating his head against a wall, looking for his own bugs -- when the *team* would spot the bug much more quickly.

There are also some ego problems if you wait too long before having a walkthrough. If one of the team members suggests that the code should be revised to make it more readable, the author of the program is likely to get quite defensive. After all, he's invested a great deal of time and energy -- psychic energy as well as physical energy -- and he's not terribly interested in listening to any suggestions about rewriting the program!

In addition, there is a psychological effect on the team: One of the things that makes a walkthrough worthwhile is finding bugs. Indeed, many organizations argue that the more bugs that are found in a walkthrough, the more successful the walkthrough. On a personal level, a programmer doesn't mind spending an hour or two of his time reviewing someone else's code if he finds a bug or two. He feels that his time has been well invested. However, if he spends an hour reading through the code and does *not* find a bug ... well, he begins to think that he's wasting his time. He begins to get sloppy, thinking to himself that there won't be any bugs in *any* code that he walks through.

9.5 Conducting the Walkthrough

In many cases, walkthroughs are so informal that one can not really say that they are "conducted." Indeed, walkthroughs are sometimes an almost personal experience -- the programmer takes someone else's code home in the evening, curls up in front of a roaring fire with a bottle of wine, and spends a pleasant evening ... looking for bugs.

In more formal circumstances, there is usually a prescribed pattern to the walkthroughs; that is, the walkthroughs tend to be "structured." What follows is merely a guideline -- to be modified as you see fit:

1. The chief programmer (if there is one) chairs the meeting and sees that order is maintained. This implies, of course, that the meeting is large enough, and formal enough -- and that the personalities are disparate enough -- that order does have to be maintained!

2. The person who wrote the code (or who carried out the design) makes a presentation to the reviewers. There is a difference of opinion on this point: Some people feel that if the design code requires an overview presentation, something must be wrong with it. It should be possible for the reviewing audience to understand it without any help (after all, that's the position the maintenance programmer will be in!). Others give a different argument: An overview presented by the author of the program is likely to "brainwash" the reviewers into making the same logical errors as the author -- and *all* of them will overlook bugs in the program. Thus, some people feel that the author should *not* make a presentation, but should be present only to answer questions from the rest of the group.

3. The walkthrough normally begins with an overview presentation. During this phase, general comments and questions may be entertained -- but specific questions ("How does your program handle an XYZ transaction?") should be deferred.

4. Following the general discussion, the author walks through the code (or the HIPO diagram, or whatever) on a line-by-line basis. This walkthrough is not usually done with specific test cases; instead, it is based on a logical argument of what the code (or the design) will do at various stages.

5. After the general walkthrough, members of the reviewing audience may ask to walk through specific test cases. This process continues as long as anyone can think of situations where the program's behavior is suspect.

6. Disagreements are normally resolved by the chief programmer, if the team itself is unable to reach a consensus. Such disagreements might include questions of style, questions of efficiency, or interpretations of the specifications ... and they tend to be of the sort that can go on interminably if they are not stopped by the meeting chairperson.

7. Additional walkthroughs may be necessary to review corrections and changes to the code. It will usually be evident whether a second walkthrough is required -- and the team should be able to reach an agreement in this area relatively quickly.

The above comments may give you the impression that walkthroughs are always formal affairs in which no one is allowed to speak unless he has raised his hand and received recognition from the chair. Such is usually not the case: Walkthroughs tend to be rather informal, give-and-take sessions among peers who need little outside supervision to maintain order.

9.6 Other Aspects of Walkthroughs

Again, we must emphasize that every organization conducts its walkthroughs somewhat differently; how your programmers conduct their walkthroughs will depend very much on their personalities and on their surroundings. However, I can offer some suggestions that seem to be generally useful in most organizations:

1. Have your programmers schedule their walkthroughs in advance -- a day in advance is usually sufficient. If possible, have them distribute appropriate materials (coding sheets, listings, HIPO diagrams) to the participants a day in advance and encourage private code reviews *prior* to the "public" walkthrough. A number of the bugs and problems that are found are trivial and need not take up the time of the entire group.

2. Make sure that you stay out of the walkthrough -- and keep any other "big bosses" out, too. You may be curious about the walkthrough mechanism, and you may wish to sit through one after your programmers have had an opportunity to get used to the technique. However, you should keep in mind that your presence -- especially during the first few walkthroughs -- will probably be extremely inhibiting.

3. See that proper notes are kept during the walkthroughs -- not only of bugs but also of suggested changes and improvements to the program. In the heat of the discussion, such suggestions tend to be forgotten ... and if the author of the program was not enthusiastic about the suggested improvements, he is *very* likely to forget about them.

4. Make sure that you create a proper attitude for the programmers: Make them see that it is *good* to find bugs. Impress upon them that *everyone* in the team is responsible for bugs: the programmer who put the bug into the program *and* the programmers who failed to find it in the walkthrough. One surefire way of impressing this point upon everyone is to make them all "sign off" the program when they are convinced it is correct -- and then call *all* of them into the computer room in the middle of the night when an undiscovered bug blows up the program during a a production run!

5. Make sure that your programmers understand that the major purpose of the walkthrough is error *detection*, not error *correction*. If the solution to a bug can be easily demonstrated to the author of the program, no harm is done -- but it is a disaster to see half a dozen programmers dash to the blackboard and begin arguing about the correctness of a "fix" that they have just invented for a bug. It is sufficient to let the author of the program know that the bug exists -- let *him* decide how to fix it.

6. Keep the walkthroughs short and sweet. An hour is long enough, and 90 minutes is probably the absolute limit. Studying someone else's code is mentally fatiguing, and one's attention begins to wander after an hour or so. And *don't* schedule walkthroughs one right after the other!

9.7 Management Problems with Walkthroughs

As you can anticipate, there can be a number of problems with the walkthrough concept. Perhaps the first problem occurs in the management area: Many EDP managers are not convinced that walkthroughs are a good idea.

Some managers, for example, argue that it's a waste of time to tie up so many people to examine code. "Six programmers sitting in a room for an hour!" a manager will exclaim. "How can that possibly be cost-effective? Chances are they spend most of their time talking about football or sex!" If you hear this complaint from other managers in your organization, you should have four answers:

1. It would probably take the original programmer considerably longer to find the same number of bugs. After all, if the programmer put bugs into his program, then the psychology of the situation is such that he will create test data that repeats

the same logical errors that exist in his code.

2. Some bugs would *never* be found by the original programmer. It's worth a few hours of time by a team to find such bugs -- otherwise, they'll be discovered in production, when they're *much* more expensive!

3. There is no other reasonable way of ensuring that the style of programming is acceptable -- i.e., that the program reflects a proper implementation of the principles of structured design and structured programming.

4. Case studies such as those discussed in Chapter 2 confirm that walkthroughs *are* productive.

You should also be prepared for the managers in your organization who feel that "all testing and debugging should be done by the computer." Again, there are some fairly standard answers that you can give:

1. Machine time is cheap compared to the cost of people -- *but*, the machine turnaround time is terrible. It may turn out that your programmers have to wait a day or two to get a program compiled -- and the chances are they aren't as productive as you think while they're waiting for that output.

2. The machine will only find bugs that the programmer is clever enough to expose with his test data. Again, it has to be emphasized that the author of the program tends to select test cases that are psychologically intended to demonstrate that his program *works*, not that his program has a bug.

3. In some cases, it may be preferable to let the computer find bugs. If the turnaround time is acceptable, it usually makes sense to let the author of the program find his own syntax errors (with the assistance of the compiler). It may also make sense to let the programmer eliminate the more trivial logic errors in his program -- but one must be careful not to wait too long for a walkthrough, or the author will become too egotistical about his code.

Still another common viewpoint is that junior programmers should not be allowed to participate in walkthroughs. Many managers feel that reviews should be done only by the chief programmers of the project. Your response to this suggestion should be:

1. The possibility of ego confrontations increases with a one-on-one situation -- particularly when it takes place between programmer and his/her superior. The team environment tends to soften the ego confrontations.

2. The chief programmer generally is too busy to give the code a really thorough walkthrough, and probably will just skim through, looking for obvious errors.

3. Even if the chief programmer spends a significant amount of time, he's only human -- he makes mistakes. Subjecting the code to a team walkthrough increases the chances that *someone* will find the bug.

4. To paraphrase the old proverb: "Out of the mouths of babes ... and junior programmers ... come pearls of wisdom." Junior programmers often have refreshingly different approaches to program design.

Finally, management is likely to be concerned about the possibility of ego problems. The programmers in their group may have very strong personalities, and the concept of a walkthrough may be viewed as an open invitation to fisticuffs. The comments we can make in this area are:

1. Bah! Arguments of this sort are healthy! Personality conflicts exist anyway. Why not get them out in the open?

2. A strong chief programmer should be able to mediate most ego conflicts, and prevent the majority of arguments from getting out of hand.

3. Many conflicts can be avoided by establishing standards at the beginning of the project. This point is discussed more fully in Chapter 12.

4. Almost all arguments can be avoided by disallowing discussions of programming style -- i.e., by restricting the walkthrough to an exercise in finding bugs. This is an unfortunate limitation, but it is better than no walkthrough at all.

5. Ego problems are easier to cope with if the review comes after a *small* programming investment has been made -- *not* after 10,000 lines of code have been written and tested by the programmer.

As you might expect, not all of the objections to walkthroughs come from the management community -- the programmers create a few problems of their own! You should anticipate the following problems when implementing walkthroughs:

1. *Attitude problems.* Some of your programmers will be unwilling to cooperate. If they can't be convinced to participate in the walkthrough approach after a few months of practice, you have two alternatives: fire them, or put them in a corner to work by themselves. If you choose the latter approach, I strongly recommend that they be forced to maintain their own code.

2. *Inexperience at giving or taking criticism.* Programmers seem to have little experience at the group dynamics required in walkthroughs: Indeed, one often finds that certain people are attracted to programming because they find it easier to deal with machines than with people. If you find this to be a problem, you should consider giving your programmers some training in transactional analysis -- the "I'm OK, you're OK" approach.

3. *Unenthusiastic programmers who don't try hard enough to find bugs.* Everyone knows about the programmer who is overly critical in a walkthrough -- he makes his presence known! What we sometimes overlook is the programmer who sits quietly in a corner and never says a word. It is worth repeating a point we made earlier: Make *everyone* feel responsible for the bug. It may help to give the quiet programmer a call at 3 AM, asking him to come into the office to help track down a bug that he didn't bother finding in the walkthrough....

4. *Walking through too much code at one time.* Watch out for this one: Your programmers will sometimes try to spend an entire day walking through several thousand lines of code. After the first hour or two, it's a waste of time.

5. *Programmers' fear that walkthroughs will be used to judge their performance.* This can be a serious problem, and you should be prepared for it. It's a rather paradoxical issue, since everyone knows that programmers are not *really* paid on the basis of their performance (as we pointed out in Chapter 7, nobody is willing to pay $100,000 for a superprogrammer). So why should a programmer care if a few bugs are found in his program? On the other hand, you can appreciate the psychological fear that the programmer has. To allay this fear, you should do two things: First, stay out of the

walkthrough, especially if the programmers view you as an ogre rather than a friend. Second, impress upon your programmers that it is the *code* that is being reviewed in a walkthrough -- not the person!

6. *Arguments over programming style.* There is no magic way of preventing programmers from arguing over the merits of nested IF statements in COBOL, or the advantages/disadvantages of a particular machine language instruction. However, the arguments are sometimes interminable -- and you should be aware of this as a problem. The best thing to do is to leave the programmers alone. Even though they may waste a considerable amount of time at first, sooner or later they will get very tired of such arguments and very tired of the time they are wasting -- and they will learn to discipline themselves. An alternative is to establish programming standards that everyone can adhere to -- but self-imposed discipline is much more effective than standards imposed from the outside.

Chapter 10 WHICH TECHNIQUES TO IMPLEMENT FIRST

The major part of our work is done now: We have discussed top-down implementation, structured design, structured programming, chief programmer teams, program librarians, and structured walkthroughs. In this chapter, we address ourselves to a question frequently asked by organizations exposed to all of the PPT techniques for the first time: *Which techniques should we implement first? Should we start with structured programming? Or would it make more sense to begin with structured design? Or should we jump in with both feet and try all of the new techniques?*

Unfortunately, there is no single right answer to these questions. What's right for one organization may not be right for another. From what you've seen thus far in this book -- and from what you know of your own organization -- *you* have to decide what would be best. Nevertheless, there are about a half a dozen things to keep in mind when deciding which PPT technique to implement first.

10.1 Trying to Implement All of the PPT Techniques at Once Will Generally Cause Chaos

Some organizations can actually pull off such a feat: After reading about the techniques, or getting a presentation from their friendly hardware vendor, they decide to use all of the new techniques at once. As you might expect, this is more likely to happen in the smaller EDP organizations -- those with only half a dozen programmers -- and is *not* very likely to occur in the larger organizations.

Sometimes, though, an organization will decide to try all of the PPT techniques on a single project; this is quite common in the case of a so-called pilot project, which we will discuss in the next chapter. Even in a limited situation like this, it usually turns out that an attempt to experiment with half a dozen new techniques at once leads to chaos and confusion.

The reasons are obvious enough. Structured programming and structured design are not simple concepts, and a lot of concentration is needed to make them work right. If the programmers are trying to implement walkthroughs -- which require a great deal of psychological energy, too! -- *and* chief programmer teams, as well as adjusting to the concept of a librarian relieving them of their clerical work ... well, it will be a wonder if they get any of it right!

This is not to say that you *can't* try all of the techniques at once; as I mentioned at the beginning of this section, some organizations *do* succeed. But most don't....

10.2 Techniques Which Involve Organizational Changes Are Often the Most Difficult

As we suggested in Chapters 7, 8, and 9, some organizations will find it difficult to *ever* implement chief programmer teams, librarians, and walkthroughs for reasons that at this point should be obvious to you. The point to be made here is that even if you *can* convince your organization to try the chief programmer team, or librarians, or walkthroughs, you'll probably find it more difficult to introduce *that* as the first PPT technique. My experience is that it is somewhat easier to introduce a relatively innocuous *technical* concept like structured programming *first* -- that doesn't threaten anyone's empire, nor is it at odds with current organizational philosophies.

Once you've demonstrated that structured programming, top-down implementation, and structured design are good ideas, *then* you'll probably be in a strong enough political position to say to the big boss, "Listen, the last three PPT techniques that I introduced to the company have turned out to be winners. Why not gamble a little now, and let me try something like the program librarian concept?"

Once again, I'm not suggesting that you *must* follow this tack. You may find that your top management is more intrigued with the organizational aspects of the PPT techniques, and is relatively uninterested in such "trivial" technical concepts as structured programming.

10.3 Structured Code Without Structured Design Is Often Worthless

We made the point earlier in the book that structured coding is a great idea (and probably a great improvement over your current approach), *but* it's not enough. If your modules are too large, you're still in trouble; if they have too many immediate subordinates (i.e., the span of control is too high), you're probably in trouble; if the modules have pathological connections or other forms of coupling between one another, you're most likely in a lot of trouble.

This point should be fairly clear to you; if not, it might be a good idea to examine the references at the end of Chapters 4 and 5. The reason I mention it in this chapter is *political:* If your organization has been doing things in a backwards fashion for years, *and* if you introduce the PPT techniques with great fanfare and promises of spectacular improvements, *then* your first PPT technique damn well better demonstrate spectacular improvements!

And if you try structured programming *alone*, you might not get such spectacular improvements. My experience on a few projects recently has been that the initial productivity and reliability will seem quite impressive, but the long-term maintainability of a system produced with nothing more than structured coding may not be very impressive at all. For a good example of this, see P.J. Plauger's article, "New York Times Revisited," in the April 1976 issue of *The YOURDON Report*.

The moral: It may make good sense to begin with structured design *first* -- and when that is working properly, *then* introduce structured coding. Once you've overcome all of the objections and battles and problems associated with structured design, it will be almost trivial introducing structured programming.

10.4 Top-Down Design and Implementation Are Often a Good Way of Introducing the PPT Techniques

As we discussed in Chapter 3, many of the advantages of the top-down approach are "political" in nature. It allows you to demonstrate something to the user at an earlier point in time; it enables you to survive deadline crises more gracefully; and it allows you to schedule machine test time in a more manageable fashion.

These benefits are *very* noticeable to the user community, to higher levels of management, to the computer operations manager, and to various other people in the organization. For that reason alone, many EDP managers have decided that the top-down approach is a good way to introduce the PPT techniques in their organization.

Keep in mind that this approach *can* backfire. As we pointed out in Chapter 3, many programmers view top-down implementation as an invitation to start coding *before* they've done any real design. Especially on your first few projects, beware of this danger.

10.5 The Most Successful Approach Has Often Been Informal Walkthroughs

Using the earlier part of this chapter as background, we can present a strong argument for informal walkthroughs as your first venture into the new PPT techniques. Note that I said "informal" walkthroughs -- not necessarily with all of the "bells and whistles" that we discussed in Chapter 9.

Why would informal walkthroughs be a good way to get started on the PPT techniques? For the simple reason that you can't trust any individual programmer to understand and implement any of the other PPT techniques *by himself*. By forcing everyone to *talk* about their designs and their code -- in a low-key, non-threatening fashion -- you can maintain some kind of quality control when you most need it.

This is a point that needs emphasizing. If you have 30 programmers, and if you send them all to a class on structured programming, they are guaranteed to hear 30 different (and almost mutually exclusive) things. They will write 30 different kinds of structured programs -- some good, some mediocre, some downright *bad*. And if nobody looks at their code (which is the current state of affairs), you'll never know who *really* understands structured programming and who doesn't.

If you begin by establishing an environment of exposing *everyone's* code to public discussion, then you'll ensure that a relatively *uniform* version of top-down implementation, structured design, and structured programming can be implemented later on.

Once again, *you* have to make the final decision. You may decide that walkthroughs -- by themselves -- are not significant enough to deserve being the *only* thing that gets introduced to your organization; you may decide to introduce walkthroughs together with structured programming or structured design.

Chapter 11 CHOOSING A PILOT PROJECT

In various parts of this book, I have obliquely referred to the concept of a "pilot project." This chapter discusses the concept in more depth.

Most organizations consider a pilot project to be a formal experiment in one or more of the PPT techniques. Indeed, that is its primary virtue: an experiment. If it should turn out that structured programming is a bad idea (despite all the good things I've said about it in this book!), it is preferable to discover that in a low-cost, low-risk experimental project. If the pilot project confirms that structured programming is a *good* idea, then the success of the project should provide the political leverage for introducing structured programming throughout the organization.

There are other benefits, too. A pilot project is a good way for people to *learn* the PPT techniques -- learning by *doing* is almost always preferable to learning from a textbook. In addition, the programmers who work on the pilot project can be used to "seed" subsequent projects when you begin implementing the PPT techniques on a larger scale.

Not every organization feels that it needs the concept of a pilot project. A small EDP organization whose members have *all* been exposed to the PPT techniques, *in depth,* may decide to formally adopt the techniques without any experimentation at all. However, most large organizations are unable to change overnight, as we suggested in the previous chapter; in such an environment, a pilot project is politically necessary to convince many programmers and project managers to try something new.

So, pilot projects are generally a good thing. However, there are *good* pilot projects and *bad* pilot projects -- and a bad pilot project is sometimes worse than none at all. The major purpose of this chapter is to offer some advice on the characteristics of a *good* pilot project.

11.1 A Good Pilot Project Should Be of a "Reasonable" Size

Some organizations make the mistake of trying the PPT techniques on too small a project. Particularly if they are experimenting with structured programming and structured design, such organizations will sometimes elect to make a 200-statement program their pilot project.

In most cases, such a tiny pilot project won't be very convincing. First of all, there's some overhead involved in the PPT techniques -- particularly if one follows the guidelines of structured design and structured programming in a formal, "religious" fashion. If nothing else, there is the problem of the "learning curve" -- by the time a programmer figures out how to use structured design and structured programming on his 200-statement problem, another programmer could have finished designing, coding, and testing it.

There is a more fundamental objection to the use of the PPT techniques on a small pilot project. Most of the PPT techniques -- particularly structured design, structured programming, top-down design, and structured walkthroughs -- were intended as a means of dealing with *complex* data processing systems. They're not needed on small problems -- we can use conventional techniques on small problems -- as indeed we have been since the 1950's. To put it more bluntly, any idiot can write 200 lines of code and eventually get it to work -- and if he has a lot of practice doing such jobs, even an idiot can write a 200-statement unstructured program faster than a programmer can finish *his first attempt* at writing those 200 statements in a structured fashion.

So, my advice is: Choose a medium-sized system as your pilot project. I would suggest a project involving three to six person-months as a reasonable interpretation of "medium-sized" ... but medium-sized should be interpreted within the context of your organization.

11.2 The Pilot Project Should Be Useful and Visible

It is probably *not* a good idea to implement an on-line chess-playing program as your PPT pilot project. Nobody will use it, nobody will care whether it is better or worse than a classical on-line chess-playing program.

It's preferable to have a project whose output will be visible to the organization, and whose success will be appreciated by various members of the organization. Perhaps a good way of stating this criterion is: The pilot project should be one that your organization was planning to implement anyway.

11.3 The Pilot Project Should Be Low-Risk

If at all possible, your pilot project should *not* be critical to the success -- or the solvency -- of your organization. Let's face it -- the project might fail, and it would be a shame if the failure put your company out of business.

To put it another way: Using the PPT techniques for the first time on a risky, highly critical project may destroy both the project *and* the reputation of the PPT techniques. The PPT techniques might turn out to be too much for the programmers to cope with -- especially if they are already coping with unreliable hardware, obnoxious customers, terribly tight schedules, and internal politics.

And if the project *does* fail, it would not be surprising to see the failure blamed on the PPT techniques -- even if the *real* reason for the failure was the schedule, or the computer vendor, or something else.

Of course, there are some cases when you might not have any alternative: If you have been put in charge of a project that appears doomed to failure, you may decide to gamble on the PPT techniques, in the hope that they will produce a miracle. I know of one or two organizations that have been forced into this position -- and, luckily, they have succeeded. But it's something you should avoid if you possibly can.

In this context, the ideal pilot project might be a redesign of an existing system -- a system that is so old, so patched, and so un-maintainable that everyone agrees it should be scrapped and redeveloped. Your new PPT version will probably be a success, and you'll have the added advantage of having something to compare it to (which we'll discuss further in the next section). Even if the PPT version should prove to be a failure, though, you can probably survive -- by continuing to use the old system.

11.4 The Pilot Project Should Be Measurable

One of the purposes of the pilot project, as we have said, is to *demonstrate* the virtues of the PPT techniques to the rest of your organization. This strongly implies that you should *measure* various aspects of the pilot project; that is, you should consider measuring such things as:

- How many lines of debugged code per programmer per day were generated in the pilot project?
- How many bugs were found after the system was put into production?
- How much *less* efficient was the structured product than an equivalent unstructured version would have been?
- How much time was spent in walkthroughs? How many bugs were found in a typical walkthrough?

These few categories may prove sufficient, or you may decide to turn the pilot project into a full-scale research project. The point is, hard *numbers* will usually convince the rest of your organization to believe the success of the pilot project.

There is one potential problem: You may not have any numbers in your organization with which to compare the pilot project. Most organizations today have no idea how productive their programmers are; how many bugs exist in their production systems; or how much effort they are spending on maintenance. As a result, it becomes difficult to tell whether the pilot project is substantially better or worse than the classical method.

One solution might be to compare the results of your pilot project with the figures that are reported in the literature -- e.g., case studies that are regularly reported in *Datamation, Infosystems, Computerworld,* and various other journals. Unfortunately, this is difficult to do, because -- as we first mentioned in Chapter 2 -- everybody seems to measure these things differently.

It is because of this that many organizations feel that the ideal pilot project is a redesign of an existing system. With some investigation, one can usually accumulate the relevant statistics about the current version of the system: How long did it take to develop? How many bugs have been discovered during the past N years of maintenance? How many maintenance programmers are assigned to the system? And, of course, there is one area where you can get *hard* statistics: How much CPU time and how much memory does the current system consume? This obviously forms the basis of a comparison with the new PPT version of the system.

The subject of "standards" comes up sooner or later in any discussion of the PPT techniques. It is *not* the purpose of this book to provide you with all the standards you'll need in your organization; however, I would like to offer some brief advice on *when* and *how* such standards should be developed.

Perhaps the first thing to say is that many of your standards won't be affected by the introduction of the PPT techniques. A number of large organizations have an immense collection of standards, much of which is unrelated to, or only peripherally related to, the issues of structured programming, walkthroughs, and the other PPT techniques. One of my clients for example, even has a standard to determine the color of the standards manual: Systems standards manuals are green, programming standards manuals are blue, operations standards manuals are yellow, personnel standards manuals are red, and so forth.... Presumably, the PPT techniques would not upset this carefully developed scheme!

Even in the area of systems design and program design, many of the conventional standards can be left unchanged. Your organization probably has standards that dictate how disk packs are used; what kind of file-names are used; what kind of paperwork has to be filled out before a job is given to the computer operator; and so forth. I would estimate that 90-95% of this can be left intact -- much to the relief of your standards organization!

There are probably only a few aspects of your standards manual that should be scrapped:

1. "Religious" rules outlawing a few isolated programming statements -- particularly COBOL standards that outlaw PERFORM's and nested IF's, and PL/I standards that outlaw procedure calls.

2. All of the emphasis on the microsecond-level of efficiency. Large portions of some organizations' standards manuals are concerned with the relative merits of COMP-2 versus COMP-3 data representation in COBOL, and the relative efficiencies of obscure string-handling statements in PL/I. As we tried to emphasize in previous chapters, this level of efficiency is usually irrelevant.

3. Most of the sections concerning packaging. If your standards dictate that systems *must* be

broken into job steps in a certain way, and that data *must* be passed between job steps on a certain kind of tape file, you should probably rewrite the standards in light of the packaging concepts of structured design -- or eliminate the standards altogether.

There are a few other suggestions that can be made about standards for the new PPT techniques.

12.1 Don't Develop Standards Until After a Pilot Project

A few organizations make the mistake of trying to develop a whole new standards manual *before* they have any real experience with the PPT techniques.

Indeed, the members of the pilot project may wish to develop a few informal standards -- mostly so they won't waste time quibbling over details in their structured walkthroughs -- but this is something quite different from a formal set of standards issued by the Standards Department.

The reasoning here should be obvious: You can't really tell what kind of standards will be appropriate until *after* you have tried the PPT techniques. How can you tell whether nested IF statements are bad until you (or your programmers) have tried writing a few of them?

12.2 "Hard" Standards Will Probably Be Ignored

As we suggested in earlier chapters, there is a tendency for some organizations to interpret some of the guidelines of structured programming, structured design, structured walkthroughs, and other PPT techniques as religious rules -- and these rules have a nasty habit of ending up in a standards manual.

Thus, I've begun seeing standards manuals that contain the following kind of statements:

- "All walkthroughs must be between 30 and 60 minutes in duration."
- "Each programmer must have a walkthrough of his code on a weekly basis."
- "GOTO statements will not be allowed under any circumstances."
- "The span of control of a module must never exceed seven."

It may be possible to force your programmers to follow these dictatorial standards for a while -- but sooner or later, they'll fall into disuse, just as the last set of "hard" standards fell into disuse!

12.3 Summary

From the comments above, you can probably anticipate the approach that I favor: a modest set of style guidelines, combined with frequent walkthroughs.

I find it intriguing that many of the organizations that have developed structured programming standards have been able to express all of their guidelines in ten or twelve pages ... and many of the managers indicated that a deliberate effort was made to keep the standards to a restricted length to ensure that the programmers would actually read them! By way of example, I have included a copy of the structured COBOL programming standards used in my company; you'll find it in Appendix A.

The thing that will really determine the success or failure of your standards is the *walkthrough* concept discussed in Chapter 9. Indeed, one could argue that if the walkthrough concept is successfully implemented, no standards are needed -- certainly not any "hard" standards.

This point has to be emphasized, particularly in the organizations that have fallen in love with their standards manuals. What is the purpose of standards in the area of program design and coding? Presumably they ensure that the programmers will turn out *good* programs! But "goodness" is something that ultimately has to be judged by a human being -- typically, the maintenance programmer who is called upon to make such judgments at 3 o'clock in the morning, when he is looking for a bug!

My point is very simple: If a team of programmers reads through the design and code for a system, and honestly thinks it is "good" -- then it probably *is* good, regardless of what the six-volume standards manual may say. And if the team thinks that the program is bad, then it probably *is* bad -- even if the programmer has scrupulously obeyed all of the rules, all of the do's and don'ts of the standards manual.

Chapter 13 THE IMPACT OF THE PPT TECHNIQUES ON SCHEDULING, BUDGETING, AND PROJECT CONTROL

One of the questions raised frequently about the PPT techniques is their effect on classical estimating, scheduling, budgeting, resource allocation, and project control -- that is, all of the things that are normally associated with classical project management.

Implicit in this question is the assumption that everything that the project manager has learned about managing EDP projects will not have to be thrown out the window -- it's assumed that with the new PPT techniques, everything will be different.

The primary purpose of this chapter is to reassure you that most of the knowledge and experience you've gained in this area is still valid. Specifically, the chapter will discuss the effect of the PPT techniques on estimating and scheduling activities; the effect of the PPT techniques on milestones as they are classically understood; and the kind of milestones that are generally used in PPT projects.

13.1 The Effect of the PPT Techniques on Estimating and Scheduling

This is the one area of the book where I have to admit to being a complete cynic. I honestly don't know how people estimate projects or how they determine when a project can be finished. I am aware that there are some very complex formulas that one can use to estimate how long a project will take, and how many people will be required to complete it in the allotted time.* And I am aware that there is a body of knowledge on scheduling of manpower for large projects.**

Nevertheless, I remain a cynic. Perhaps this is because of my experience as a consultant: I have seen, time and time again, that people are unable to come up with reasonable estimates *because they are working on a programming project of a type that they have never worked on before.*

---

*See, for example, the discussion in George Weinwurm's *On the Management of Computer Programming,* Auerbach Publishers, Inc., Princeton, N.J., 1970.

**See Philip Metzger's *Programming Project Management,* Prentice-Hall, 1975.

Example: Charlie-the-programming-manager has just been placed in charge of a new on-line order entry system, to be developed on a Brand X computer, with a Brand Y data base management system and a Brand Z telecommunications monitor. The only kind of order entry system that Charlie ever worked on before was a smaller, simpler batch system that ran on a Brand W computer, using a different programming language and different programmers. How is Charlie to come up with an accurate estimate?

In many cases, Charlie doesn't have to come up with a schedule: The schedule is determined for him. Part of the assignment is " ... and get this damn system up and running by the first of January!" Charlie then does the obvious interpolation between where he is now, and where he must be by January first: "Let's see, now... this is April 1st, and I have four programmers, and I've gotta be done by January 1st ... that means that I'd better have the design finished by June 1st, and I better start coding by July 1st ... and ... and ..."

You may not agree with all of this. You may have your own tried-and-true method of estimating and scheduling systems -- in which case I congratulate you, and suggest that you keep your method secret, and guard it as carefully as you would a winning method for betting on the stock market or the horse races! You might even consider becoming a consultant!

All I am saying is that *I* don't know how to estimate projects in a scientific, rational, error-free manner. And I suspect (though I'm not enough of a cad to actually say it) that you don't either.

I *do* know this, though: However you've been estimating and scheduling your projects, you should continue to do it the same way with the new PPT techniques -- with the possible exception of the "fudge factor" that you used to apply to your estimates. That is, your present scheme might involve asking programmer Fred for an estimate of the time required to program module X. If Fred estimates that the job will take him 13 days, your normal tendency might be to double that -- because you know Fred is outrageously optimistic. And then ... and then you add a fudge factor of 50% to cover unforeseen circumstances. With the PPT techniques, there's a good chance that you can eliminate the 50% fudge factor, though you'll want to continue compensating for Fred's optimism. Indeed, for the first few projects (e.g., during the pilot project discussed in Chapter 12), you should even continue to include the 50% fudge factor....

What I'm really saying, then, is this: *Continue estimating your projects just like you used to.* If you have a scientific method of scheduling your projects, fantastic! -- keep doing it! If you schedule your projects according to a combination of your horoscope, the stock market average, and the phase of the moon, keep doing it!

The effect of the PPT techniques on all of this should be fairly simple: *The chances are that you'll be able to meet the schedule and the estimates that you make.* And that's not a trivial statement! With your current projects, you double Fred's estimates, add 50% just to be safe -- and yet the project is still three months late! With the new PPT techniques, your scheme should be to double Fred's estimate, add 50% to be safe -- *and then meet that schedule.*

Think about it for a minute: *Why* are your current projects three months late? Aside from totally unforeseen catastrophes, what is the cause of the schedule slippage? Chances are it's not the time required to design the system, nor the time required to write the code. Most of the slippage occurs during that nebulous period of time called "system test and integration." And *that* category -- which you probably never scheduled for in a properly conservative fashion -- is the one that will be decreased significantly with the new PPT techniques.

Lest you think that I am being unnecessarily cynical, let me reassure you that I, too, make an honest attempt at scheduling and estimating the computer systems I become involved with. How? Probably the same way you do -- by breaking the system into small enough pieces (i.e., modules) that each piece is assigned to an individual programmer, or a very small group of programmers. Then I ask each programmer -- or small group of programmers -- for an estimate ... and I adjust their estimates up or down based on my knowledge of their performance. And then I add up all of the estimates from all of the programmers, throw in another fudge factor or two ... and *voila!* I have the overall estimate for the project!

With the PPT techniques -- and particularly with structured design -- I have every reason to suspect that this process will be more accurate. First, the structured design approach tends to favor smaller modules (which are easier to estimate accurately); second, it tends to favor highly *independent* modules (so that the overall effort for the project is more nearly approximated by the sum of the individual parts). In the past, the estimates tended to be based on larger modules (whose completion was more difficult to estimate accurately), and on modules which tended to be more *dependent* on one another (a fact which often wasn't discovered until systems integration!).

13.2 The Effect of the PPT Techniques on Classical Milestones

In the past, data processing projects have had a number of recognizable milestones:

- request for system received
- approval received to begin system study
- system study completed
- specification for new system completed
- specification for new system accepted
- computer systems design for new system completed
- detailed module design completed
- coding completed
- unit test completed
- system test completed
- acceptance test completed
- system in production

Each milestone was an opportunity for various members of the organization to gather together and review the status of the project. If the milestone had been achieved on schedule, and within the budget constraints, everyone assumed that the project was proceeding according to plan.

With the new PPT techniques, many of these classical milestones will disappear. How *many* of the milestones disappear depends upon whether you elect the conservative top-down approach or the radical top-down approach (recall the discussion in Chapter 3). If you elect to follow a conservative approach, all of the milestones *up to and including* "detailed module design completed" will remain the same.

If you elect to follow the radical approach, you can expect the first three milestones listed above to remain the same -- that is, *up to and including* "system study completed."

Sooner or later, you should expect to see the influence of the PPT techniques on your milestones (sooner if you follow the radical approach, later if you follow the conservative approach): an integrated pattern of specification *and* design *and* coding *and* testing.

What we are saying is very simple: With the PPT techniques, you may expect that some design (and even some specification) will be taking place all the way up to the day before the deadline. You can expect to see your programmers writing code on the day before the deadline. These are things that would have caused ulcers if you were following the classical approach -- because you would expect such coding efforts to be followed by several months of that ill-defined activity known as "system test and integration."

13.3 The Nature of Milestones with the PPT Techniques

I suggested in the previous section that many of the classical milestones will be eliminated with the PPT techniques. If that is the case, what kind of new milestones will take their place?

If you recall the discussion of Chapter 3, the answer should be obvious: The milestones correspond to the delivery of various *versions* of the system. Actually, the first few milestones will be the same as they are in the classical approach: We are usually required to produce a "system study," and we may (in a conservative approach) be required to produce a detailed design of a proposed new system.

Sooner or later, though, our milestones can be expressed in terms of "versions." What gives the PPT approach such a tremendous advantage over the classical approach is that the versions can be defined in terms of (a) a definite date of implementation, and (b) definite features and capabilities that it will be able to perform.

Consider, for example, the simple payroll system that was discussed in Chapter 3. We could imagine the following set of milestones -- assuming a slightly conservative approach:

January 1	--	request for new payroll system received
February 1	--	approval received to begin system study
March 1	--	system study completed
April 1	--	specification for new system completed
May 1	--	version 1 payroll system in operation
June 1	--	version 2 payroll system in operation
July 1	--	version 3 payroll system in operation
August 1	--	version 4 -- the final version -- in operation

The advantage of the "version" milestones is that they are *tangible*. Remembering our discussion of the payroll system in Chapter 3, we recall that version 1 (a) would not hire anyone or fire anyone, (b) could not give anyone a salary increase or decrease, (c) paid everyone $100 per week, (d) withheld $15 per week in taxes, and (e) paid everyone with a paycheck printed in octal. Version 1 can thus be defined in terms of tangible characteristics -- *and version 1 either works, or does not work, on the specified deadline.*

It is this last point that is so crucial. With the classical method of project management, a typical milestone would be described as "detailed module design completed." But what does that mean? How do we know that it has been accomplished? How do we know that some design problems have not been postponed, to be discovered at some later milestone?

It is interesting to see what happens at each milestone of a PPT project. When the deadline arrives for version 1, for example, there is a non-trivial chance that the system will not be working -- in the case of our payroll system, *the programmers will be unable to produce an octal paycheck for $100.*

"Oh, but that's not fair," the programmers will complain. "Actually, we're all done -- it's just that there's this one little bug that's preventing us from getting the right output."

To which the project manager replies, "Too bad! You're not done! You didn't meet the deadline!"

And the programmers cry, "But that's not fair! We're 99.7% done! All we have is one last bug! And we think the bug is in the compiler!"

And the manager, stern-faced devil that he is, replies, "Too bad! As far as I'm concerned, version 1 either works -- or it doesn't work. Evidently, your system is incapable of producing octal paychecks for $100 -- so it doesn't work!"

At which point, one of the programmers might say, "But that's not fair! *My* module works just fine! It's Fred's module that's causing all the trouble!"

To which the manager replies, "I don't care whose fault it is.... Version 1 does not work! Therefore, the entire project is behind schedule. And if it isn't working by next weekend, you'll all be thrown off the Empire State Building...."

And the programmers, who insist on having the last word, say, "Geez, boss, couldn't you at least make it the World Trade Center?"

All humor aside, the version approach to milestones is *extremely* powerful. If you define your versions carefully (particularly by defining the version in terms of completed modules on a structure chart), things are much more tangible -- at a much earlier stage in the project -- than they used to be.

13.4 Summary

The message of this chapter is:

1. Prepare your estimates as you always have.

2. Expect that the first few milestones -- the administrative ones -- will be much like they always have been.

3. Get rid of the rest of your milestones, and replace them with *versions* of a top-down systems implementation.

Perhaps someday we really *will* be able to schedule and estimate computer projects realistically. On the other hand, I don't think we should feel too guilty -- nobody else seems to do a very good job either. People have been building airplanes for nearly 75 years, and yet we can't schedule and estimate most of the current military airplane projects with any degree of accuracy. People have been designing buildings for thousands of years -- but you need only talk to the people involved in the Sydney Opera House, or the Montreal Olympics, or a two-story ranch house in Dubuque, to learn that even *they* can't estimate things all that accurately.

Chapter 14 WHAT WILL GO WRONG?

This chapter is intended as a brief summary. Throughout this book, I've tried to point out the hundreds of *little* problems that you'll encounter when you begin to implement structured programming, structured design, and the other PPT techniques. But, on a larger scale, what disasters should you expect? What major failures lie in wait for you? On a philosophical level, *what will go wrong?*

The major point that I would like to make is that *none* of the PPT techniques are magic: Things *will* go wrong. Structured programming will not produce miracles. Structured design will not improve your sex life. Structured walkthroughs will not reduce the number of cavities in your children's teeth. Top-down implementation will not make it significantly easier to get along with your boyfriend/girlfriend/husband/wife/mistress/lover/dog/cat.

Having said that, we are still left with the question: *What* will go wrong? I think you should be prepared for four major problem areas -- which we will discuss below.

14.1 Most of Your Problems Are ANALYSIS Problems

Most of the discussion in this book has concerned programming, program design, and system design. It is quite possible that when you have solved all the problems in these areas, you will still be left with the fundamental problem of *trying to find out what the user wants.*

Indeed, there is something rather ironic about the whole PPT area: It has been developed bottom-up! First, structured *programming* was introduced to the world. And then -- when the world began to see that programming was not *the* critical problem -- structured design was introduced. And now -- now that we realize that the main problem is figuring out what the user wants us to do -- structured analysis is being introduced to the world.

Structured analysis could be regarded as a formal, rigorous methodology for communicating with the user and expressing his/her needs in a concise, precise form that can be understood by user, analyst, and programmer. Significantly, it makes use of many of the tools and techniques that were developed for structured programming and structured design -- but that's the subject of another book!

In the meantime, the PPT techniques will be enough to keep your data processing organization busy for a while. Just keep in mind that when you've digested all of the PPT techniques, you'll still have some work to do.

14.2 Your Programmers May Turn Out to Be Too Dumb to Learn the PPT Techniques

Anyone who has been in the computer field for ten years or more tends to have fond memories of "the good old days." Those were the days, the old-timer will tell you ... those were the days when everyone knew how the compiler worked, how the operating system worked, and even how the hardware worked -- you *had* to, because you generally had to patch all three on a day-to-day basis to get any work done. Those were the days when people worked around the clock, slept in the computer room, operated their own programs....

Naturally, there is a certain degree of exaggeration in these stories -- but there is an element of truth, too. In particular, one gets the impression that in "the good old days" people lived to program -- whereas today, people program to live. For a majority of computer programmers today, it's just a job -- something to occupy them from 9 to 5, something that enables them to pay the rent and buy two color TV's.

I suspect something happened to the personality and the mentality of the programming profession -- as a whole -- as we moved from "the good old days" to the super-sophisticated on-line, real-time, fourth-generation 1970's. I suspect that the profession began to attract people who, regardless of their race, creed, color, or university degrees, are *clerks*. They think like clerks, they talk like clerks, and they approach computer programming with all the enthusiasm of a sleepy Civil Service clerk who knows that he's just one year away from retirement.

What's the point of all this? My observation of the average programmer -- having met some 10,000 of them throughout the world -- is that a surprising number of them have *never* read any computer articles; have never opened *Datamation* or *Computerworld;* have never heard of ACM, DPMA, IEEE, ASM, or any other professional organizations; can't spell Dijkstra's name, and probably have never heard of him; haven't heard of the PPT techniques, and wouldn't be interested if they were shown the techniques.

What if such programmers were *forced* to learn structured programming, structured design, and top-down implementation? I'm sorry to say that a frighteningly large number of them are unable to learn the PPT techniques -- in addition to being *uninterested* in their profession, a frightening number of programmers are *incompetent* at their profession. It's literally all they can do to write programs in the disorganized helter-skelter fashion to which they have become accustomed; to suggest that they should introduce some organization, some common sense, some *structure* into their work -- that is beyond their ken.

If it sounds like I'm taking potshots at *your* organization, I apologize; yours may be one of the organizations with *good* programmers. My experience has been that small organizations -- especially those that *must* make a profit on a year-to-year basis to survive -- tend to have good programmers. And conversely, my experience has been that large, stagnant, conservative organizations -- those which basically survive by inertia, by *being,* without necessarily making a profit -- tend to attract incompetent programmers; unfortunately, that description fits a lot of big banks, insurance companies, government agencies, and super-big manufacturing organizations.

If it sounds like I'm damning the entire programming profession from some lofty perch, I apologize again. However, it discourages me to meet programmers who have been programming in COBOL for ten years, and who have no idea how a PERFORM statement works -- and who are considered among the brightest in their organization!

14.3 Your Organization May Take a Long Time to Begin Using the New Techniques

Even if your programmers are of average intelligence, you may run into another problem: It can easily take two or three years for the effect of the PPT techniques to be felt in your organization. On a global scale, this is very easy to illustrate: Structured programming was introduced to the world in the 1965-68 era, was widely discussed in the available literature in the 1969-73 era, and was formally hailed by *Datamation* as "the greatest invention since the subroutine" in December, 1973. And yet, there are many organizations that *still* have not done anything about the PPT techniques.

Why? Well, the reasons vary from organization to organization, but there is a certain pattern that becomes very familiar. First of all, nobody in company X heard about structured programming for a long time because they were so busy working on current projects -- nobody read that issue of *Datamation,* nobody went to any computer conferences, nobody talked to anyone in any other companies.

And when they *did* hear about structured programming, they weren't quite sure what to do about it. It was probably brought to their attention by the hardware vendor -- and everyone suspected that structured programming was really a subtle plot by the vendor to sell more memory or another disk pack. After a while, someone decided to set up a committee to study the relevance of the PPT techniques to their organization -- and the committee studied it for six months before reporting anything.

Once the committee decided that structured programming was a good idea, someone made a copy of a *Datamation* article for all of the programmers -- with a memo that said, "The boss thinks this is a good idea." The programmers ignored it for several months. Another memo was circulated; this one said, "The boss wants everyone to use structured programming from now on."

At that point, the programmers began writing *their interpretation* of structured code. It didn't work; they didn't like it; the COBOL compiler wouldn't compile it. So they ignored it again, knowing that the boss never read their code anyway.

Having seen that the effort was getting nowhere, someone then decided to take a more organized approach. Some of the brighter programmers were sent to a training course, or given a book to read, or put in front of a videotape machine. A pilot project was attempted -- and when it finished with mediocre results, a *second* pilot project was attempted.

Assuming that the pilot project was eventually successful, standards were developed (everyone knows how long *that* takes!). Meetings were held among all the project managers; structured programming was declared officially to be a "good" thing. Everyone was told to get organized, get trained, and begin really *doing* structured programming.

Some project managers demurred: They were in the middle of a critical project, and they couldn't afford to rock the boat with any newfangled ideas. "*Next* project," they promised, "we'll start using structured programming." Other project managers objected to the PPT techniques for the various political reasons we've outlined throughout this book.

Meanwhile, *some* managers actually *did* begin using the PPT techniques on a large scale. But no results were forthcoming -- it was a three-year project, and nobody really wanted to believe the results until the *end* of the project.

How long does all of this take? A year? Two years? Five years? I've seen a few organizations switch to the PPT techniques overnight, but most of the larger ones take anywhere from one to five years to begin seeing *real* results. And meanwhile, during that period, you've got to keep suffering with bugs, low productivity, maintenance headaches, and so forth....

14.4 Maintenance Problems

The final problem area is one that we've mentioned several times in the book: Even with all the new PPT techniques, you still have to maintain the accumulated programming garbage of ten or twenty years.

I don't have to tell you how much fun it is to maintain an IBM 1401 AUTOCODER program on a 370/168 -- especially when the listing and the source program for the 1401 program were lost long ago, and all you have is a patched object module. There are some organizations that have *hundreds* of such rotten, old programs.

If you're one of those unlucky managers who is stuck with the maintenance of 1,000 man-years of unstructured code, there's not much I can do for you -- other than offer you a lot of sympathy. Sympathy, and one last little bit of advice: If you don't start *now* to write your new systems in a structured fashion, you'll be in the same position ten years from now.

APPENDIX

Suggested Standards for Structured Coding in COBOL

Introduction

The prime objective of this style guide is the production of readable structured code from a structured design of independent function modules. The standards are not intended for mechanical enforcement, but to serve as a point of departure for each software development group in deciding what will and will not be acceptable in code reviews.

TOPIC: PROCEDURE UNITS

STANDARD: The basic procedure unit is a paragraph; several paragraphs may be packaged into a section, especially if their functions are temporally bound, e.g., initialization functions.

'JECTED ALTERNATIVES:

1) Basic unit is a section.
2) Basic unit is a separately compilable entity.

DISCUSSION:

A module is defined as one or more code statements together fulfilling a single function, with one and only one label by which it may be invoked.

The COBOL construct which most nearly satisfies this is the paragraph. Using the section as the basic unit with no paragraph names has been recommended, as some compilers would then enforce the discipline of an EXIT statement. This is not the case in ANS 74 COBOL. An EXIT statement should only be provided if required as the target of a GO TO within the procedure.

Having a separately compilable entity as the basic unit, with no labels inside each entity, is possible and gives excellent interface clarity, but the repetition of Data Divisions makes for less readable source code.

We envisage micromodules (paragraphs) being packaged into macromodules (compilable entities) by the program designer after completion of the structured design. Where segmentation is important, or in certain forms of case structure, paragraphs may be packaged into sections.

It is implicit in the definition of a module that, no matter what level in the hierarchy, it should have only one entrance (the label) and one exit.

Control should never be allowed to pass implicitly across any procedure name, i.e., it should not be possible to "fall through" from one procedure to the procedure which happens to be physically next in the code.

Micromodules should be marked off visually from each other by a blank line before and after.

The size of a macromodule (program) is not critical from the point of view of readability. It may be desirable to have separately compilable entities for changeability, and there may be constraints on main storage size.

TOPIC: PROCEDURE NAMES WITHIN A MACROMODULE

STANDARD: Each procedure name should express the function of the procedure and should have a prefix, of a letter plus a digit, which gives its relative location within the Procedure Division.

This prefix may be omitted from Procedure Divisions covering less than two pages.

REJECTED ALTERNATIVE:

Use of a suffix.

DISCUSSION:

Where the micromodules form a hierarchy, they should be numbered A1-A9 for the first level, B1-B9 for the second level, for example:

```
          PERFORM A1-INITIALIZATION.
          PERFORM A2-PROCESS-RECORDS.
          PERFORM A3-WRAPUP.

      A1-INITIALIZATION.
          .
          .
          .
      A2-PROCESS-RECORDS.
          .
          .
          .
          PERFORM B1-READ-RECORD
            UNTIL ALL-DONE.
```

TOPIC: DATA NAMING AND DEFINITION

STANDARD:

1) Data names should be as meaningful as possible while not being overlong, and should be given a suffix if they are used in the macromodule interface, -IN for input, -OUT for output.

2) Working storage will consist of a level Ø1 for each micromodule, with the suffix -WS. Working storage used by that micromodule will be defined under this Ø1.

   Shared working storage will be defined as Ø1 COMMON-WS.

3) No micromodule may modify another module's private working storage.

4) The VALUE clause is used only to establish parameters and tables that never change. As much as possible, variables should be initialized in the procedure division, near where they are used. The need for initialization should be kept to a minimum.

5) Hyphenation should be used to add meaning, e.g., CD-MF-AC-NO rather than CDMFACNO.

6) Only counters and binary flags may be coded as literals. All other numbers other than Ø and 1 are suspect as literals and such numbers should be coded as initialized variables with meaningful names. Ø and 1 should be given names where they represent "true" or "false" or similar condition values.

7) The use of level 88 names should be avoided, as it obscures the relationship between the setting and testing of flag values. Instead, make free use of numeric parameters for such values; e.g.,

```
IF RECORDS-LEFT = NO

MOVE YES TO DONE
```

TOPIC: STRUCTURES

STANDARD: *Process structures:* concatenations of instructions normally involving no transfer of control within the structure, e.g., MOVEs, arithmetic, I/O.

Exception conditions (AT END, ON SIZE ERROR, etc.): If dealing with this condition is part of the function of the module, insert the necessary code. If the function should be dealt with by one of the calling modules, set a flag, or better still use the normal output data parameters to pass back exception information.

A concatenation of structures can normally be treated as a simple process structure, except when it is under control of a conditional statement (e.g., IF, READ ... AT END) and the concatenation of structures must contain an imbedded period. In this case, the process structure is written as a separate paragraph and PERFORMed.

Decision structures: The normal layout is:

```
IF  condition-1
    imperative-1
ELSE
    imperative-2.
```

Where the logic demands a nested IF (i.e., an imperative is replaced by another IF) the structure should wherever possible be rewritten in the "linear" form:

```
IF        condition-1
            imperative-1
ELSE IF   condition-2
            imperative-2
ELSE
            imperative-3.
```

NEXT SENTENCE should be revised out of the code wherever possible, even if it means introducing a NOT. Avoid mixing AND and OR in a condition; if you must do so use parentheses to make it unambiguous.

Where the code implements a decision table, include the decision table as comments.

Where IFs must be nested, each level of IF should be indented, and its corresponding ELSE aligned with it. (An obvious exception is the ELSE-IF chain above.)

As far as possible, the code for a condition should follow the usage of normal speech; if a condition is not comprehensible when read aloud, it should be recast.

CASE structures: where a single variable may take more than two values and a different procedure must be performed depending on each value.

For non-numeric variables, use the linear chain of ELSE IFs; for example:

```
    IF       CODE = A
                     PERFORM PROCEDURE-A
    ELSE IF CODE = B
                     PERFORM PROCEDURE-B
    ELSE IF CODE = C
                     PERFORM PROCEDURE-C

    ELSE
                     PERFORM ILLEGAL-CODE-ROUTINE.

         .
         .
         .

PROCEDURE-A.
         .
         .
         .

PROCEDURE-B.

         .
         .

PROCEDURE-C.
         .
         .

ILLEGAL-CODE-ROUTINE.

         .
         .
         .
```

For *integer* variables it is permissible to use a GO TO ... DEPENDING ON within a Section, for example:

```
CASE-STRUCTURE SECTION.
SET-CASE-SWITCH.
    GO TO PROCEDURE-1 PROCEDURE-2 PROCEDURE-3
                DEPENDING ON CODE.
PROCEDURE-1.
    .
    .
    GO TO CASE-STRUCTURE-XIT.
PROCEDURE-2.
    .
    .
    GO TO CASE-STRUCTURE-XIT.
PROCEDURE-3.
    .
    .
    GO TO CASE-STRUCTURE-XIT.
CASE-STRUCTURE-XIT.
    EXIT.
```

This whole section is PERFORMed from an appropriate place in the program.

Never contrive a code just so that you can use a GO TO ... DEPENDING ON ... Unless the code arises naturally in the data representation, use the linear chain of ELSE IFs.

Loop structures: For multiple executions ending on a condition (zero or more times)

```
PERFORM loop-proc
    UNTIL condition.
```

For multiple executions ending on a condition (one or more times)

```
PERFORM loop-proc.
PERFORM loop-proc
    UNTIL condition.
```

For multiple executions on a counter value (zero or more times)

```
PERFORM loop-proc
    VARYING counter-name
    FROM    initial-value
    BY      increment
    UNTIL   condition.
```

ALTERNATIVES REJECTED:

PERFORM THRU: This leads to confusion and implies that a functional entity can be addressed at points inside itself. If you need to write PERFORM PROC-A THRU PROC-C, write a "sandwich" procedure, consisting of

```
SANDWICH-PROC.
    PERFORM PROC-A.
    PERFORM PROC-B.
    PERFORM PROC-C.
```

Then PERFORM SANDWICH-PROC as needed.

PERFORM n TIMES: This encourages the use of literals. Use PERFORM ... VARYING instead as this will show the exit point more meaningfully.

DISCUSSION:

Note that there are three uses for the PERFORM statement:

1) to invoke a sub-module, which performs a complete function and returns (procedure call).

2) to invoke a process block which cannot be written in-line (group).

3) to invoke a loop body zero or more times (loop).

Therefore, not all paragraphs may be complete functional modules in the sense of structured design; some may be groups or loop-bodies, i.e., sequentially or even procedurally bound modules.

TOPIC: LOOPS WHICH READ SEQUENTIAL FILES

STANDARD: MOVE YES TO RECORDS-LEFT.

```
READ the file
  AT END MOVE NO TO RECORDS-LEFT.

PERFORM the loop
  UNTIL RECORDS-LEFT = NO.
```

At the end of the loop's code READ again to get the next record.

REJECTED ALTERNATIVES:

```
MOVE YES TO RECORDS-LEFT.

PERFORM the loop
  UNTIL RECORDS-LEFT = NO.
```

As the first step in the loop

```
READ the file
  AT END MOVE NO TO RECORDS-LEFT.
IF RECORDS-LEFT = NO
  body of loop
  .
  .
  .
  .
```

DISCUSSION:

From the design point of view, it is preferable to carry out an initial read and set a flag, since if the file is empty, the executive module can deal with this condition straight away. The alternative puts the body of the loop as a series of clauses within the positive branch of an IF statement.

TOPIC: EXPLICITNESS

STANDARD:

Arithmetic. Do not write a COMPUTE of more than three variables/constants: Break any more complex equation up into intermediate steps.

Notation. Do not use > < : Some people find them confusing and some print chains do not have them.

Format. Align all related verbs.
Align all PICs (col. 32 is suggested).
Align all VALUEs (col. 44 is suggested).

TOPIC: COMMENTS

STANDARD: Use comments (* in col. 7) where the code has to do something which is not self-evident, or is not directly related to function. This usually occurs where the pseudocode cannot be converted directly to COBOL, e.g., in a swap. Consider rewriting any code that needs explaining.

Include any decision tables you develop as comments immediately before the decision structure which implements them.

If the gross function of the macromodule is not clear from reading the highest level micromodule, include pseudocode for the macromodule as comments as the first thing in the Procedure Division.

Include a comment wherever a variable is modified whose values have level 88 condition names, or wherever data is modified by more than one micromodule (unless the data is in COMMON-WS).

Use comments to explain *what* code is doing, not *how* it is doing it.

In general, imagine that someone else is writing this code, and in the middle of the night next week *you* will have to pick it up and make a change to it under pressure of time.

Write unto others as you would wish to be written unto.

TOPIC: FORMATTING

STANDARD:

1) Only one statement or procedure name per line.

2) UNTIL, AT END, ON SIZE ERROR, VARYING, and similar qualifying clauses should be indented two spaces from the verbs they qualify, e.g.,

```
READ CARD-FILE
  AT END MOVE NO TO CARDS-LEFT.
```

3) Each ELSE should be directly under the IF to which it refers, except in the case of linear ELSE IF sequences.

4) Where a statement is so long that it must be broken, break it at a word so that it is obvious that the statement must be continued.